The Joy of Growing Up:
Growing Up for Grownups
Who Haven't Grown Up Yet

Wendy Freebourne MSc

Bright Pen

Visit us online at www.authorsonline.co.uk

A Bright Pen Book

ISBN 0 7552 1029-8

Authors OnLine Ltd
40 Castle Street
Hertford SG14 1HR
England

This book is also available in e-book format, details of which are available at www.authorsonline.co.uk

'There is no birth of consciousness without pain.'
C G Jung (1925)

About the Author

Wendy Freebourne MSc was born in 1947 in East London, where she started her education, mainly in the University of Life. She first learned about codependency in her family. She left school at sixteen and qualified as a Chartered Accountant. When her two sons were born, in the early seventies, she became involved with alternative medicine and ran a hospital in Hampshire for five years. This led her to retrain as a Psychotherapist. She has been working with individuals, couples and groups for twenty-five years. She is also a practising astrologer. In 1998 she was awarded an MSc in Psychology for research into relationships at the University of Lincolnshire and Humberside. There, and at Leeds University, she also studied Systemic Practice. 'I am fascinated by the dynamics of relationships,' she says, 'the patterns that emerge and repeat themselves.'

Wendy has also studied and practised Tibetan Buddhism and several other spiritual disciplines and has travelled in Europe, North Africa and India.

She has produced a series of CDs, The Dependency Talks, dealing with recovery from codependency, dysfunctional families and the underlying cause of dependencies and addictions; and a psycho-spiritual astrological report, Pathfinder Workbook. She has also had magazine articles, short stories and poetry published. Currently, she has a novel about relationships in progress and is taking herself seriously as a textile artist.

Further information about Wendy's work can be found at:
http://www.relationshipscentral.com

Contents

Foreword

I heard about Wendy Freebourne's work with dependency in nineteen ninety-four and finally got to meet her the following year, when a group of us tracked her down and invited her to run some workshops in York.

What I learned from her tried and trusted methods reached beyond dependency and gave me an awareness of and insights into my own personality. Her methods have also helped me in my work as a counsellor and research scientist in the field of addictions.

Wendy and I worked together with couples and groups during nineteen ninety-six and ninety-seven. The experience of her deep understanding of human development and relationships has since given me healthy outcomes I had not anticipated in dealing with difficult addicted inmates in United Kingdom prisons, sometimes in dangerous circumstances. This experience has also helped in dealing with intricate staff relationships. Wendy's elucidations of how and why we function within a sometimes highly dysfunctional world and how we can do that more effectively have led me to revelations, research and new training opportunities.

When Wendy first talked to me about writing this book, she was intending to write about relationships, but I suggested that her work is, in fact, about more than that; it is about how to grow up in the twenty-first century.

Fraser Trevor MSc
Middlesbrough, England
July 2005

xi

Acknowledgements

My special thanks for inspiration, help and support in writing this book go to Hans Thomsen, Ronnie Moehrke and Fraser Trevor, who gave me the original idea; as well as the members of the Bath Writers' Group on whom I tested the early chapters. I thank Oliver Gilson for his technical support and Justin Gilson for the space to write it in. I am grateful to Jenny Hewitt for careful editing and advice and to Wendy Lake and the staff at Authors OnLine for holding my hand through the publishing process. I am indebted to all those brave souls who attended the Dependency Workshops from nineteen ninety-two to nineteen ninety-six and who helped me to establish and clarify some of the basic tenets on which this book is based. I also appreciate those writers and thinkers I have quoted, whose words inspired me and echoed my own thoughts.

Introduction

> *'I cannot tell the truth about anything*
> *unless I confess being a student,*
> *growing and learning something new every day.*
> *The more I learn, the clearer my view of the world becomes.'*
> *– Sonia Sanchez*

Although we talk about growing up, in fact, apart from growing to your full height, you do not grow *up*; you just become more of who you are. Up is not a place where growing comes to an end, where you are all complete and perfect. Growing is a life-long process. However, for the purposes of this book, I use the term 'grown up' as the dictionary defines it, to mean adult, or mature, although some adults are more mature than others. I also use it to describe a feeling and a temporary, but recurring, state of being.

That feeling of *being* grown up makes me happy. I feel real, at home with myself and glad to be me. I feel capable and, while I have that feeling, complete. I have a sense of achievement. For me, maturity is a good feeling.

This book is my attempt to share these feelings with you, to explain to you that *being* grown up can be a joy. I want to share with you that part of my view of the world that has become clearer. I think, in many ways, being grown up has had bad press and maturity has not been given the respect it deserves. As a child, I got the impression that being an adult meant responsibility, which implied burden and hard work, and that meant suffering. I often heard 'getting old' used to explain tiredness, weakness and infirmity in older people.

At the same time, being grown up promised to be a magical state I would one day attain, when I would be able to do all the things I seemed to be unable or forbidden to do as a child. I was impatient to grow up. But I was also confused. For me, as an adult, growing up has been, and continues to be, a struggle at times, because of a lack of adequate models. I have had to find these models for myself and now hope to share them with you. I have learned that becoming grown up does not happen at any one time; it is an ongoing journey.

As I have worked as a psychotherapist with my clients, and with myself, for more than twenty-five years, I have come to understand that responsibility chosen carefully and taken on willingly brings freedom and fulfilment. I now know that our physical abilities do change as we get older, but this does not mean that illness and infirmity are necessary results of aging.

I have seen many people using models of dependency to manage the responsibilities of adulthood, and continuing to believe they are still as helpless as they were when they were children. I have also seen extreme models of independence, which I call pseudo-independence, that are both proud and defensive. In my experience, these models are unproductive and ultimately work against you. I have come to understand that they are used to fend off the feelings of powerlessness and inadequacy that come with dependency. Until I learned that, as an adult, I am not powerless, helpless or inadequate, I also felt these feelings. I learned, and am still learning, how to use my adult resources fully and effectively. I am still growing up.

I have seen how these models can be handed down through generations. However it is possible to create your own models for going further than what may have been the limitations of the previous generation, even if you have to make similar mistakes to them along the way. I find there are always new lessons to learn in life and new things to try. No parents or teachers could have taught you all you need to know anyway; and life would be so boring if they had. For me, part of the joy of growing up is experiencing it as it happens, at various stages of my life.

In this book, I explain how adult dependency and pseudo-independence keep you enmeshed in the past and burdened in the present. They also limit you in what you can expect in the future. With these models you age, but you are much less likely to mature.

This book is an attempt to show you how to enjoy the freedom that comes with true independence, which allows you to interdepend with others. As you grow, you gradually develop your resources, physical, emotional, intellectual, as well as spiritual; from the cutting of your first tooth, your first step, to the struggle for separation and independence, which reaches its peak at adolescence, stepping out into the world and earning your living; and then learning to live with other people, becoming sexually active, partnering and possibly raising your own children too. If your models for using your resources are immature and inappropriate to your current age, you find yourself failing in what you want to do. I aim to teach you simple, practical and workable skills, so you can enjoy using your resources more effectively.

In Part One I look at the processes of growing and changing. Then I attempt to identify, differentiate, clarify and illustrate dependence, which is natural and healthy and belongs in childhood; then independence, which is the healthy, gradual separation from childhood and the gaining of autonomy; and lastly interdependence, which is the sharing of this independence and autonomy through mutual support and exchange of resources. Thus dependence is used throughout to represent immature dependency and interdependence to mean mature dependability. Dependence, independence and interdependence are the stages I now believe you need to grow through before you can truly experience being grown up.

I use the word 'immature' to describe behaviour that more appropriately belongs in childhood, which is not grown up yet. I do not mean this as a judgement. Most of us use immature behaviour at times.

Part One will enable you to see not only where you can go, and how, but also where you have been in getting to where you are today. I explain why you might want to cling to dependency, compensating by overly asserting independence, yet avoiding maturity and responsibility. I also describe the disadvantages of adult dependency and also pseudo-independence, neither of which, in my experience, allows you to develop yourself completely. You will see what you sacrifice by remaining dependent and feigning independence. I hope you will be able to use my description of growth, change, dependence, independence and interdependence as a map to understand *your* process of growing.

In Part Two, I offer you what I see as the benefits of being grown up and explain how to use these as resources in your life now. By explaining what being grown up is, I will attempt to show you how to live in the present, understand the past and take practical steps to realise your dreams and visions in the future. It is my intention that the illustrations in this book give you models for maturity that enable you to make the transition from feelings of helplessness and inadequacy to feelings of personal power and integrity, demonstrating the many gifts, joys and advantages you can enjoy as a mature adult.

Having dealt with the practicalities, in Part Three, I address the spiritual implications of growth and potential and the urge towards wholeness, linking this to your self and your soul, and the child that you once were, to your relationship with your own divinity as a fragment of that divinity that is the whole you may understand as God, or the Universe.

Throughout this book, I share stories of how the pain of helplessness and dependency and the loneliness of pseudo-independence can be healed and how the transitions between dependence, independence and interdependence can be completed smoothly at any time. I have had the privilege of witnessing, supporting and facilitating the growing up processes of many people. These stories are a combination of some of their experiences. They also include my own experiences in learning how to grow beyond the age when the models available to me appeared to become redundant; ineffective in supporting a creative and fulfilling adult life.

My key to growing up joyfully, youthfully and effectively is to learn to manage change and live through uncertainty. I offer you tools to help you allow uncertainty, develop flexibility and face the future creatively, with more confidence and less anxiety.

I am not a great believer in theory that is not grounded in experience, which I value. I believe that our personal truth lies in what we experience and our experience comes from what we feel. No one can take this truth away from you, even though they, and you, out of necessity, may deny it. I believe that, ultimately, this truth is your authority, without which you cannot have integrity, both of which are essential elements of maturity.

It is my intention for you to use the ideas I put forward, gleaned from my own experience, as tools, rather than theories, to help you enjoy being fully mature. These ideas form the foundations on which this book is based and I will develop them gradually. I hope they will be useful to you.

I work with psychology because it gives me models for understanding what motivates us and makes us tick. I believe in rationality, in using intelligence and analytical ability, which are not fully present in childhood but develop with age and experience. Above all I see this development of logic and reasoning ability as a gift of adulthood, which is often under or misused. I also see it as being the greatest difference between being an adult and being a child. Even though many children would appear to reason more adequately than many adults, they usually do not have enough information available to them to come to adequate conclusions.

Lastly, a word about behaviour; in this book, I do urge you to change strategies that no longer work for you, which, of course, means changing behaviour. I explain how certain behaviours defeat you. However, in my experience, changing behaviour alone is ineffective; (it is a short-term measure only), if your current experience is being influenced by emotions that you were not able to acknowledge, manage or effectively express in the past, and decisions which are determined by the immature and distorted interpretation of those emotions. So, from time to time, I may suggest that you examine your motivations. Your early experiences may be colouring your interpretation of your present feelings and current experience. I will make suggestions for interpretations that are likely to be more appropriate to your present age and understanding and give you tools for channelling your emotions creatively, rather than destructively.

> 'The important thing is this:
> to be able at any moment to sacrifice what we are
> for what we could become.'
> – Charles Du Bos

Part I

Becoming Your Own Person

1

YOU DON'T GROW *UP*

> *'And the day came when the risk to remain tight in a bud*
> *was greater than the risk it took to blossom.'*
> *– Anaïs Nin*

What Do I Mean By Growing?

Growing is a lifelong process of becoming more of who you are. You gradually blossom, expanding and extending yourself on all levels, the physical, emotional, intellectual and spiritual. It is natural that you want to do this because it gives you the pleasure that comes from achievement. You feel yourself being stretched by the challenge of going further than you have been before. This is exciting. However, it may mean taking some risks, facing the unknown, living through periods of transition and uncertainty and allowing changes to happen. I will explain how to manage change and uncertainty in the next chapter.

Moving from Comfort to Pleasure

> *'Without a sufficiently secure base, we feel anxious;*
> *without the opportunity to explore, life is boring.'*
> *– Lavinia Gomez*

Taking risks means leaving what feels safe, because it is familiar. It means exploring something new. This is the way to greater independence and maturity. Safety and familiarity may feel comfortable, but they can become uncomfortable, restricting and stunting, even suffocating and painful; something you grow out of, like a pair of shoes that have become too tight for you. Safety and familiarity can also become boring and frustrating. Then growing becomes more appealing. Even if you are apprehensive at first, it ultimately gives you pleasure. In order to grow, you need to make choices in your life. As you grow older and more capable, you no longer need the kind of safety you did before. You can choose between comfort and pleasure. If you are stuck between the two because you are afraid to move forward, then you need to look at your security, inner and outer.

What You Need to Grow

You need security to grow effectively, to be able to take risks, to be spontaneous and creative. Children need dependable caring and parenting, and a stable environment to grow up in. If you have had this, you are more likely to be a secure and stable person. You are more likely to be capable of finding and creating a consistent and dependable social environment; one that supports and contains you and your life; one that allows you the stimulation and challenge you need to grow, as well as the freedom and flexibility to go on growing. If you have had genuine warmth and love in your childhood, you are more likely to be a warm and loving person; able to care for yourself, nourish yourself and get the additional nourishment you need from your adult environment and the people in it; then you will have inner, personal security and outer, social security. If you were loved, you will feel confident in what you do. You will believe in yourself and your abilities. In subsequent chapters I will explain how you can parent yourself now and make your adult environment safe and supportive.

If your adult environment supports maturity, your life is more likely to be satisfying, even if it is challenging. If it encourages dependency, then you may have comfort, but you will have less chance of fulfilment. Many of you may reach an acceptable level of happiness this way, but you may not reach your full potential. If you are reading this book, I suspect you want more.

Jackie was a woman of thirty who realised she wanted more. Her symptoms were telling her that.

An Acceptable Level of Happiness

Jackie came to see me with an eating problem she had since childhood, which was currently disrupting her life and affecting her relationship with her husband. She had several qualifications, a good job, a generally happy marriage, a large house and a comfortable lifestyle. But she could not control her eating and swung compulsively between dieting and overeating. She also overworked, over-exercised and obsessed about housework. Jackie was thin and slight, with a large head and big eyes. She looked like a hungry and undernourished child.

She told me her father had a successful business. When she was little he worked long hours to build it up and her mother helped him. They were hard workers. Jackie thought the business had been more important than her and her twin sisters, who were eighteen months younger. When the twins came along, Jackie got even less attention from her mother who admitted, years later, that she had never wanted to be a mother, but her husband wanted a family. Jackie comforted herself by eating, hiding food away in her room at night. Her mother would compensate her children by feeding them large meals, and then worry that her daughter was overweight. Later on, Jackie was encouraged to diet.

We started by looking at some of Jackie's behaviours, but, after a while she admitted she was not happy in her successful commercial job and wanted to work in the helping professions, where she could better use her science qualifications. But this would mean a drop in the salary she believed she needed to support her lifestyle. Jackie realised she was working in commerce to please her father, who had paid for her education. She thought she had to repay him by working hard and proving she could live to the standard he had set for himself.

She also realised she was unfulfilled, like her mother, who had devoted her life to her husband and his business. 'She never thought about what she wanted for herself,' Jackie told me. Jackie realised she was using food and work to fill up the emptiness she felt inside. With my support, she gave herself permission to have what she wanted. She took steps to change her career. She thought she had not wanted children but realised she did. So did her husband. By agreeing to share childcare, they found they could both work part-time and also care for a child, which pleased Jackie. Her husband agreed they could move to a smaller house in a less expensive area where they would also have family nearby. Jackie's parents were, in fact, supportive of her doing this.

Jackie created models that were different from those her parents had; models that supported what she wanted for herself and were also compatible with what her husband wanted. These models helped her balance her personal and professional life and have the best of both worlds. Her obsession with food disappeared. She gained balance in her weight too and lost her hungry look. Consequently, her periods, absent because of her dieting, returned and she was able to conceive. She said she felt happy, even though she was no longer depending on the things she had been taught would give her happiness: food and work and lifestyle. Although these had given her comfort at first, they had ended up causing her discomfort, restricting her freedom and creativity. She had originally used them to comfort herself when she was hurting, but they had eventually become the cause of her pain.

> Remember:
> Comfort may ease pain,
> but it does not address its cause.
> It can ultimately become its cause.

Normal or Healthy

What is accepted as normal may be stable, but I do not believe it is healthy if it does not promote growth and allow for change. I intend to show you that happiness exists beyond what you may think is your socially accepted norm and that it is possible to reach for it. I will show you how to do this, without sacrificing your relationships or your security, but in fact, by improving them. You will see that, as a mature person, you can make choices about, and contributions to, the society that you live in. You can choose to live in an environment, social and material, that supports your growth. You will also see that there is a difference between stable, predictable, dependent, but limiting personal and social relationships and mature, interdependent but less predictable ones. Growth happens in cycles. During cycles of healthy growth, it is possible to keep a balance between stability and change.

For You to Think About:

Your present environment, material and social, and how it supports your growth.

> *'Be not afraid of growing slowly; be only afraid of standing still.'*
> *– Chinese Proverb*

2

WHAT IF?

> *'I've learned that you'll never be disappointed*
> *if you always keep an eye on uncharted territory,*
> *where you'll be challenged and growing and having fun.'*
> *– Kirstie Alley*

Change is the Only Thing that is Certain in Life

Change can be refreshing and fun. Everything in nature changes as it grows. Growth is healthy and creative; it brings new life. If you are open to change, you will be adaptable and flexible and more likely to grow. You will have more chance of living your life fully and coming to its end, a transition, naturally and healthily.

Although change is certain, its outcome is often uncertain. This can make you feel insecure and, therefore, less open to it. If you are resisting and trying to maintain the status quo, you are likely to be more rigid and controlling; you want to cling to the past. In the last chapter I talked about safety. It is not particularly safe to try to prevent development and evolution from happening. If you cling to the past you are less likely to grow up. If you are rigid and controlling, you have more chance of ageing prematurely, because you are stagnating.

Change is natural. You can expect it to happen from time to time and recognise it as an opportunity to grow, to grow up more and so feel more secure. For me, growing up is basically about how you learn to accept and manage innovation, variety and diversity. Resisting prevents you from growing, although it may work for you until something outside your control forces change to happen. Then your resistance can create a crisis because you have not *taken* control, (not the same as controlling), by managing change; it is managing you. The effect is more distressing than it would be if you were already prepared for the likelihood of shifting events, impermanence and the need to move on.

> *Change need not mean ending.*

Your Resistance to Change Can Create a Crisis

Nick found this out in his marriage.

> Nick was in his late forties. He came to me because his doctor had diagnosed depression, which was affecting his work. His second, unsatisfactory marriage had recently ended. His wife kept saying she was unhappy with the relationship. Nick told her, 'I don't want to talk about it.' If she pushed him he became hostile and verbally abusive. She withdrew from sex but nothing changed. On her instigation, they moved into separate rooms. Nick retreated more and more into himself, and his work. He told her he was happy with the existing situation and still saw them as a couple. He convinced himself that sex did not matter. His wife eventually exploded and asked him to leave. Nick was deeply shocked by this confrontation. When he came to see me he was living alone and had more or less withdrawn from life.
>
> Nick told me he could not cope with emotions. He did not know how to deal with his wife's unhappiness. I explained to him that, by ignoring the need for change in the relationship and refusing to discuss it, he had precipitated a crisis. He agreed that the effect was traumatic. We looked at how he has cut himself off from what he was most afraid of losing, love and belonging, and that this was why his wife had gradually withdrawn from him.
>
> Nick had a lonely childhood. He had no siblings. His parents were actors, travelling a lot, so he was brought up mainly by his maternal grandparents. When they died, he was sent to boarding school. He only saw his parents for short periods. In the holidays he went to various relatives or to families of school friends. He never felt he

belonged anywhere. Not knowing how to behave in a family, he usually got himself into trouble and was often asked to leave. He never made connections with people. In his marriages he repeated what he knew.

Nick associated changes with endings and separations, so he tried to maintain the status quo, even if that meant ignoring what was happening around him. The more he ignored his wife, the angrier, more dissatisfied and detached she became. He created what he was familiar with, not what he wanted because, he told me, he believed he would fall apart if he allowed himself to feel anything. This is how he felt as a child when there was no one to hold him.

Nick and I spent a long time looking at change and how it had been too frequent in his childhood for him to build inner security. We also looked at the many ways in which change had also been a positive force in his life, ways in which it had worked for him. We used this positive model of change to help him build better models for managing his present life, including mapping out what he wanted in that life, so that he could have some hope for the future, rather than allowing himself to stagnate, as he was doing.

Like Nick, you may find that you are using childhood experiences as your expectations in the present, when your adult experience has already taught you something different. You are more likely to revert to childhood expectations when you feel pressured. And you are more likely to feel pressured if, like Nick, you ignore the need for change until it has built up into a crisis.

Living with Uncertainty – Transitions

> 'Change is the constant, the signal for rebirth,
> the egg of the phoenix.'
> – Christina Baldwin

Change involves transitions, between the known and the yet-to-be-known. These can make interesting and stimulating journeys, but can also throw up insecurities. Transitions are times of uncertainty, but also immense learning opportunities. You may experience this uncertainty as chaotic and confusing because what has become inflexible and outworn in your personality, your life or your relationships is disintegrating, because it no longer serves you. Before you label this as a bad experience, consider that you do not need what you feel you are losing, even though it may be painful to let it go. In fact, it may be working against you. Disintegration is part of reorganisation, so that, like the phoenix rising from the ashes, something new can form, reintegrate and consolidate. This is how you gain greater integrity. And greater integrity leads to not only more complete maturity, but also expanded opportunities and choices, even if you do have to give up what was once comforting and familiar. You are getting something better in exchange. Learning to recognize, respect and tolerate uncertainty is part of the healthy process of growing up. It helps if you accept it as a fact of life and know that you will not be uncertain forever.

The unknown can be exciting and enticing, but not knowing can also feel uncomfortable and frightening. The outcome of change is uncertain, because it leads to the future and you cannot know the future in advance. If, like Nick, you are afraid of change, you are likely to use what you already know to try to control what you do not yet know, by attempting to predict outcomes of unfamiliar situations. At the best you can only predict possibilities. If you are mature enough, you will base these predictions on adult experience and information. Otherwise you may base them on what I call 'distorted thinking' – acquired beliefs, imagination and uninformed assumptions. You do this by projecting what you have understood, assumed, or been taught in *your past*, into what you do not yet know, *your future*. This is not always reliable.

In this way you try to create the experiences you had in the past, in the future, simply because they are known and familiar, which feels comfortable, even though they worked against you; and because you insist on knowing the future in advance. The future will always reveal itself in time, if you are patient. I have found that the future is more often an improvement on the past.

> *There is no shame in admitting that you do not know.*
> *You can always come to know what you do not know now.*

What is familiar may feel comfortable, but what you do not yet know you can have, because you have never had it before, brings something other than comfort; it brings pleasure, satisfaction and fulfilment, even if you have to endure the discomfort of not knowing while you are waiting for it to materialise. Growing up is not always comfortable, but it is satisfying and fulfilling. Growing pains are very different to shrinking pains.

New Models for the Future

You will be more willing to let go of the past if you can substitute new models for the future, models on which you can more accurately base your prediction of possibilities, rather than attempting to guarantee outcomes. In my experience, we do not want to let go of one thing until we have another to take its place. For myself, on any journey, I like to have a map.

Fergus built some new models for himself in therapy.

> Fergus, in his early forties, came to see me because he was so anxious about his life. It had become chaotic and he could not see where it was going. He wanted a map. He wanted to extricate himself from a demanding and immature relationship with Clara, his wife of many years, which he was aware was dependent and did not fulfil his adult needs. He was also engaged in legal proceedings with his ex-employer, believing he had lost his professional credibility because of his boss's incompetence, even though he had chosen to resign from his job in

order to make changes in his life anyway. Although he had moved away to start a new life, he continued to see Clara, and to fight with her. He also continued to battle with his ex-boss.

Fergus was preoccupied with how his parents had been. He said they were immature, incompetent, withdrawn and afraid of life. He told me they expected loyalty from their children, but found it difficult to engage with them. He said he did not know how to be grown up. It seemed to me that, in a lot of ways, Fergus had made a good job of growing up. He was competent in many areas of his life.

I encouraged him to confront his anger towards his parents. In this way he was able to see the difference between them and himself. He was also able to see that what they had struggled with was different to what he was struggling with, even though he was doing it in the same way they had done; he was using their models. He realised he had far more resources than he had when he was in his family, and that he is not inadequate, even though he believed his parents were. Daring to challenge their models for life has helped him to build his own models of maturity, suitable for his present age, experience and resources. In this way he has been able to let go of his childhood and move on. This has also helped him to let go of two fruitless and destructive relationships.

Now that he understands how responsible he felt for his mother, who had difficulty meeting either her own or his needs, and how angry he felt about this, Fergus can understand how he has remained tied to Clara through guilt, while also feeling angry with her. He also understands that he is not responsible for her happiness and has been able to separate from her. He accepts he can now provide the gracious and pleasing lifestyle that Clara gave him, and that he valued, for himself, even though he never had this as a child.

And since he has learned to articulate his anger towards the father who did not give him the guidance he wanted in life, Fergus has been able to stop blaming his ex-employer and take responsibility for the choice he made, at the same time understanding the validity of that choice. Validating his choices, and his right and ability to make them is enabling him to start a new career and a new life.

Fergus has managed his transition by learning several models for maturity.

To Better Manage Uncertainty

To better manage uncertainty you can:

- Change your perceptions to fit your present circumstances.
- Use logic and reason to check out whether your current feelings are appropriate for your present age, experience, abilities and your current situation.
- By using your current understanding to better interpret your emotions, decide whether your original interpretations are more appropriate to the past, when you really were helpless and dependent.
- Use the resources you have now, that you did not have as a child.
- Challenge beliefs that you were taught and ask yourself what you believe now.
- Check out the logic of your beliefs.
- Gather information so that you are better informed in your decision-making.

This is what I helped Fergus to do.

If you find you are being exhausted by conflict and confusion, then something in your life needs to change. You can choose to use the resources you do have to initiate this change.

You can welcome change as a friend.

Because I like maps, I have learned to chart my own journey, listening to my inner needs and observing how I grow, just as I would with a child. I watch for what works for me. This takes time and patience but has yielded some useful tools for coping with life in a realistic way, new models that I can use in the future.

```
Remember:
If you take the express train
you are likely to miss the scenery.
```

Living *through* uncertainty, allowing it to be until it clarifies, which it will, in time, brings new experience, new learning, knowledge and maturity. Clinging to what is certain is often narrow and limiting. Certainty can also be an illusion, because change is inevitable at some time.

Coping Methods

If you grew up in conditions that were less than adequate to support your growth, you may have invented coping method to survive. These inventions were ingenious and probably worked for you in a limited and dysfunctional environment. However, if you have based your expectations for the future on adverse and dysfunctional experiences in the past, you are likely to use those same methods of coping because they are familiar to you, even though they are no longer appropriate. The paradox is that, because they are not functional behaviours, in the present they become ineffective and have EXACTLY THE OPPOSITE EFFECT they had when you first adopted them. They keep you:

- trapped in the past
- scared
- dependent
- feeling small
- and inadequate
- and probably alienating people in your relationships

because they are based on the assumptions you made as a child, within the limitations of your childhood environment and experience, and with the limited resources and information available to you then. These coping methods prevent you from growing up and fulfilling your potential. They prevent you from getting what you want because they are designed for merely coping, not fully living.

However, they do keep you safe from taking risks or responsibility.

This is what was happening to Nick and to Fergus. But, when they examined their coping methods, they found that calculated risk-taking and responsibility gave them more than survival, they gave them real life, hope and freedom, as well as increased faith in the future.

I recommend that you examine your own coping methods from time to time and assess whether they are working for or against you.

For You to Think About:

What expectations your life is based upon.
What is distorted in your thinking.

> *'If we don't change, we don't grow.*
> *If we don't grow, we aren't really living.'*
> *– Gail Sheehy*

3

SOME ADULTS ARE MORE MATURE THAN OTHERS

> 'But childhood prolonged, cannot remain a fairyland.
> It becomes a hell.'
> – Louise Bogan

What Is Dependency?

Childhood definitely has its joys, but I wonder if you would want to stay there forever. Although some people manage quite well with ongoing immaturity, I have seen others entrenched in adult dependency, not knowing how to grow out of it, and suffering.

I have heard childhood described as the best time of our lives. Although it is a very good time, I am not sure this is entirely true. It is great to be looked after when you are a child, but it is also limiting, frustrating and even painful to be helpless and incapable.

When you were tiny, you could not do anything for yourself. You were dependent on other people for your survival. You needed them to take responsibility for you, to the extent that you were not yet able to take responsibility for yourself. This gave you a special kind of freedom, for a while. But you did not have the benefits that taking responsibility brings. Your ability to make choices and decisions for yourself was limited. You may have had blissful naivety, but you did not have the ability to gather information on which to base your decisions. There were many skills you had to learn. Until you did, you were dependent.

As you got older, you would have been allowed, encouraged and enabled to grow more capable, self-sufficient, mature and independent. You gradually learned to do more and more for yourself. You were also capable of, encouraged and allowed to take on more responsibility.

Your control of yourself and your life was limited to the extent that other people took responsibility for you; they therefore had a degree of control and authority *over* you. As you took on more responsibility, you were allowed more authority and more control of your own life. How this process was managed, or not, has influenced how you learned to become an adult.

What Are Dependency Needs?

I call these dependency needs because you are dependent on other people to meet them when you are a child. You do not have the capabilities and choices you have as an adult.

Your survival needs are:

- Food, water and air.
- Shelter and protection.
- Warmth and clothing.

Without these you would die. As a baby, at least, you were not physically able to get all of these for yourself.

You also need:

- Love
- Attention
- Social interaction
- Positive regard – acknowledgement, recognition and affirmation

for your spiritual, emotional and psychological well-being. Initially, you needed other people to provide these for you and to respond appropriately to your natural love, sociability and emerging sexuality.

And:

- Intellectual stimulation
- Education and information

in order to develop and use your ability to think for yourself. You will find it difficult to grow out of dependency if you are not used to having these. You will not be equipped to make rational and informed decisions as an adult if you cannot use your intellect and gather information. You will feel powerless without at least basic education.

Plus:

- A sense of connection to yourself.
- A sense of belonging, of being part of something bigger than you.
- A sense of meaning and purpose to your life.

This is your spiritual connection and orientation, which many of you may spend much of your adult lives searching for. If your early environment did not enable you to feel spiritually connected to yourself and to feel part of something else, then, as an adult, you may search for these things externally, through adult dependency, through other people, rather than, initially, within.

Believing In Helplessness and Dependency

> 'The reason we fail to cope is not that we lack the capacity to do so but that we are <u>unaware</u> that we have such capabilities.'
> – Abraham J Twerski MD

Many adults still believe they are dependent. They also believe they are helpless in many areas. As an adult you do need other people, but not in the way you did as a child. You have more capabilities and more choices than you did then. You may not be aware of the choices you have until you are challenged to look for them. As an adult, many of your basic needs are similar to those you had as a child, but you are more capable of fulfilling those needs yourself; and of choosing and interacting with appropriate people to help you fulfil them. You are not dependent on any one person and you are more capable of self-dependence.

As an adult:

- You may still feel dependent, when you are not. If you still feel like a child, you may not have grown up yet in the way you are handling emotions. That is why I recommend checking out your feelings in the present to see if you are currently being influenced by and acting out emotions you never expressed adequately in the past.
- You may still feel dependent because you lack the tools for growing up.
- Or you may have learned tools that you are not using.
- You may not want to behave like an adult because you benefit from staying dependent: you do not have to take risks or responsibility and you do not have to make choices. In this way you can live your life through someone else. You can blame them when things go wrong and, when they do, you can believe you are a victim.
- In the end you pay a price for staying this way. You forfeit the benefits of growing up: freedom, authority, power, and control of your life.

Dependency is limiting.

> We all fall into patterns of dependency at times, specially when we are stressed.

You may also fall into helplessness as a response to stress because you are used to believing in your helplessness without questioning it.

Adult Dependency

Like many people, you probably feel empty at times and long for something you cannot always name. This is when you are searching for your connection to your self and trying to find a life that fits that self. Without these feelings you might not strive for more. After all, hopefully, you are growing and learning and achieving new objectives all the time. This striving is to know who you are and to live it through self-expression in many ways.

If your childhood needs were not met well enough, you may still be trying to get some of them met now. If you did not have good enough examples of maturity, you would not have learned over time to meet those needs yourself. You will be looking to other people to do this for you, to fill you up. You will probably have what I call the symptoms of adult dependency, to a greater or lesser degree. This means you are uncertain about who you are and what is your reality. You look to other people to define these for you. Also, you try to build your life *through*, rather than *alongside*, other people's.

The result is that you compromise your integrity by complying with other people's wishes in order to please them, so they will meet your needs; and by trying to control them in order to ensure they do this. (This kind of compliance is also an attempt to control). The paradox is, in trying to find a self and a life this way, you actually sacrifice your self and your life. You do not have a life of your own and you do not express who you are through that life. Fergus did this with Clara. It is difficult for you to grow up and develop your own potential this way because you do not know who you are and cannot assess your own resources. You go on feeling empty. You look for comfort from the pain of emptiness in another person. This often leads to more pain.

In my experience, you will be happiest when you are able to be your authentic self. Compromising separates you from your truth, and therefore your self. You may have a sense there is another you, but not know how to get to it. As well as emptiness, the pain of this separation from your self generates longing, which you project onto someone else and then fall in love with them, hoping they will heal your pain and make you feel complete. In the end you feel even emptier because this is not really love; it is a form of narcissism, which does not fill you up. It is your self you are longing for – to be whole, real and authentic. The other person cannot fulfil this for you. As they are probably dependent and compromising too, they will not be genuine with you.

Nor can you project your self onto a god or guru, or into religion or spirituality. If you are in pain and feeling empty, this is in fact a means of denial and, sooner or later, you will have to deal with what you are denying: the loss of your sense of self.

> *'You've got to do your own growing,*
> *no matter how tall your grandfather was.'*
> *– Irish Proverb*

You do need your own integrity to be grown up and to be genuinely spiritual. It is important not to compromise it. You cannot feel whole or complete through someone else. And you do need a life of your own. Nor can you have authority when you are compromising your own reality, because your authority comes from that inner place of knowing that reality.

Addictions – To Fill Up the Emptiness

Transferring your dependency onto other people is called codependency. This is a form of addiction. So is love addiction, which is really the longing for your own lost soul, your self. You may also transfer your dependency onto substances (alcohol, drugs or food), behaviours (shopping, gambling, obsessing, working, rage, sex) or objects (life styles, material possessions) in various other forms of addiction. If you are doing this, you are *using* someone or something else to fill up the emptiness, and the holes in your integrity. As I said, you can also *use* religion and spirituality. It is growing up and learning mature love that ultimately fills these holes.

Addictions are an attempt to fill yourself up from the outside, rather than from your own resources. They are also an attempt to kill the pain of separation from your authentic self. This separation happens when you have not had the adequate nurturing and parenting that enables you to learn to be who you are and to use your resources effectively; when you have had to compromise in order to adapt to your parents' limitations. Incomplete separation from your parents, caused by limited parenting, is the cause of your dependency. You are unwilling to separate because your needs have not been adequately met. You are still waiting for this to happen.

It is only to the extent that you are connected to your own soul and owning and using your resources that you can share them with other souls. If you are not happy with yourself, you will not be happy with someone else. Even though you may use other people to get 'high', these highs are only 'fixes', ego strokes that boost your self-esteem; they do not last and you crave to repeat them with increasing frequency. As they become less and less effective, you demand more and more. This is the nature of all addictions.

In adult dependency, you look to others to compensate for what you feel is missing in yourself, rather than to complement what you already have, which is *interdependence*.

The growing up tools in this book help you to use your resources more effectively.

Remember:
Anyone who attempts to keep you dependent,
to rob you of your ability to take responsibility for yourself,
is depriving you of the experience you need to grow.

They are also trying to control you.

Fergus's Story

Fergus believed in his helplessness. He was searching for his true self. He was also rescuing Clara from taking responsibility for herself. Let us look again at their complicated relationship.

As a child, Fergus did not have his dependency needs properly met. His mother did not know how to relate to him as one might with a small child. She treated him as an extension of herself. She would confide in him as if he were an adult. She was also ill a lot. Fergus believed he had to comply with what his mother needed him to be. He interpreted this as being still, quiet and helpful. He told me he believed he had never had his childhood. I believe he spent his childhood merged with his mother and her needs. Not only was he alone and unloved, but he also had no separate identity.

Although he had been successful in his adult career, Fergus still felt like a child, which he disliked; yet he still craved the childhood he never had. This was because he believed his needs would not be met as an adult. He confused his childhood needs and experiences with his adult needs and experiences. He still felt dependent on Clara, even though he had left her. Although the relationship was limiting, he complied with her wishes, even though he did not want to. He sacrificed his maturity so she would look after him when, in fact, he was looking after her. He believed he had done this with his mother as a small boy. This gave him the illusion of being nurtured and having an identity, but also kept him feeling helpless and dependent, when, in fact, he no longer needed looking after. He then felt he could not escape from Clara, that she had power over him, which she did not. This was making his life a mess.

Guilt served Fergus well, because it kept him tied to Clara so that he would not have to face his fear of being alone and feeling abandoned as he had done as a child. Yet he was abandoning himself. He kept insisting that, all his life, he had never felt real or genuine; trying to convince me he was a phoney. He knew there was another part of him and he wanted to get to it; but he did not know how.

Fergus was afraid to stand on his own two feet because he believed he did not have any feet to stand on, so to speak. He had no sense of his own self or his reality. This is how he had always felt. When he felt helpless and powerless, because of his dependency, he indulged in compulsive behaviour, obsessing about what he had lost, his job and his marriage, and immersing himself in self-pity. He became angry with himself. This was debilitating. He was sick and anxious and could not earn his living. The more anxious he became, the more he would cling to Clara, which made him more anxious because he could not be himself with her, which made him feel unreal. He was caught in a vicious cycle. This is how it is with adult dependency.

Fergus had learned not to be angry with the parents he depended on in case he upset them. They told him they were doing the best they could so he rationalised that his anger was unjustified, even though it was genuine and indeed real for him. At first he was afraid to confront this anger in our sessions, where they could not hear him or retaliate. Only when he had done this was he able to feel real and allow that other, genuine but buried part of himself to emerge, gradually, and to build models to enable it to function in his adult life. After that he felt secure enough in his new-found reality to stop clinging to Clara. Fergus stopped compromising himself and started allowing her to take responsibility for her own life. He also stopped destroying himself and started to use his time and energy more creatively, grieving for the childhood he never had and then letting it go. Having learned to believe in himself and to be authentic, Fergus began to accept and enjoy being alone, independent and individual.

Dependency Can Create Social Stability

To an extent, dependency is socially acceptable and considered normal; although, what is normal may not necessarily be healthy. Dependency can be useful because it binds people together in relationships, which promotes stability, if not growth, and gives you, through its familiarity, some kind of predictability. It does not make waves. This works well for a lot of people. However, do not mistake familiarity for intimacy, which is often lacking in dependent relationships.

Dependency also indulges your natural inclinations towards comfort, safety and feelings of security; but it does not address your deeper desires, for growth and fulfilment of your full potential. In other words, dependency can hold you back, in the helpless and powerless state of childhood. This also makes you more manageable by those who might want power and control over you because you are less likely to challenge their authority. This way you make few bids for autonomy, or freedom.

For You to Think About:

Dependency in your life and how helpless you believe you are.

> *'Depend on no man, on no friend but him who can depend on himself.*
> *He only who acts conscientiously toward himself,*
> *will act so toward others.'*
> *– Johann Kaspar Lavater*

4

REACHING YOUR FULL HEIGHT

> *'Only free men can negotiate;*
> *prisoners cannot enter into contracts.'*
> *– Nelson Mandela*

Independence – Separating From Dependency

Independence gives you freedom. It also gives you an identity. While you are limited by dependency, you are not really free. As you grow in your abilities, physical, mental, emotional and also spiritual, you begin the process of separating, first from your mother, then your parents and then from your family. You are progressively able to do more and more on your own, to gradually meet your own survival needs, to think independently, know who you are, ask for what you want, tolerate, contain and articulate your feelings and eventually to manage your sexuality. This natural process happens in stages, over time. Sooner or later, you will want to establish a life of your own, your own social circle and possibly a separate family unit.

I believe you are born with an inherent sense of who you are, but you need this reflected by your environment and the people in it for it to develop and mature; and for you to believe in who you experience yourself to be. If your environment does not reflect your inherent self, you adapt in order to fit in, to survive; as I have said – to cope. Then you experience your adapted or false self and not your authentic self. You have a sense of pain and separation, which you probably do not understand and which manifests itself as anything from a vague longing to intense unhappiness. It can feel like a hole inside you.

If your early environment failed to reflect you, you search for your authentic self in other people. If you do not believe in who you experience yourself to be, you feel anxious. You do not have inner security because you are not grounded in your own reality; like Fergus, you feel unreal and phoney, even though, through denial and inflated ego, you may delude yourself into believing in a false identity. You do not trust yourself, which is even more important than trusting other people, because people are fallible.

However, if your environment supports you, you develop an authentic sense of self, make a life of your own, separate from, although, with every possibility, remain connected to, your family and you feel independent. Through the love, attention, social interaction and spiritual connection you have in your family, you learn to love yourself, pay attention to what you need, socialise and feel spiritually connected to yourself and others. This is how you gain autonomy, how you grow to feel complete and whole.

> 'There are two lasting bequests we can give our children:
> One is roots. The other is wings.'
> – Hodding Carter, Jr.

In the years around the age of fourteen, you reach an important transition in your life – adolescence. You are looking outside your family for peer support. You have been feeling the physical, emotional and psychological effects of intense changes in your body, including your emerging sexuality. You may feel like both a child and also an adult. At this age you are likely to want the independence and freedom of being an adult, without giving up the dependency and comforts of childhood, or taking on the responsibilities of maturity. It may be, at this time, that you feel ill-equipped and inadequate. You may not have all the models you need for maturity. Even if you have had good models, this is the time for exploring and learning for yourself, often by trial and error. Life can be daunting, but it also becomes a big adventure, one that goes on throughout your life, because there is always more you can learn.

Each separation is a transition. It involves change, and a degree of uncertainty. If you have developed inner security, you will move through these transitions more easily and be prepared to let go of the people who originally represented security for you. You will grow up more easily. This process will continue as you go on growing through the rest of your life. If you have not had adequate models or security, you will be more likely to struggle with new ventures, new beginnings and fresh transitions. As many of us do, you will have to find your own solutions.

If you have not had enough outer security, you will either cling to dependency, or you may try to separate forcefully by asserting your independence before you are ready – or both. Some of you may have been pushed out of the nest too soon, and others may have broken away from your parents in rebellion because you felt limited or restricted by them or that they were trying to hold on to you too tightly. In the absence of adequate models for maturity, you may have struck out to find your own, using an immature model – adolescent rebellion.

If sexuality was not contained or was suppressed and denied in your family, you may be using yours inappropriately or inadequately.

What Is Independence?

> 'The most important thing that parents can teach their children
> is how to get along without them.'
> – Frank A. Clark

Independence gives you autonomy. This means you become:

- self-directing
- self-sufficient
- self-contained
- self-reliant
- self-supporting
- and free

You have an identity, including a gender identity, a sense of who you are and strong personal boundaries. You gain authority through learning and experience. This is how you become your own person. You are not dependent on another person to complete you or to compensate for what is lacking in you. You feel whole and at home with yourself. You have inner security.

If you are deprived of learning and experience, it is hard for you to become independent; you are likely to remain dependent. You may compensate for feelings of inferiority, inadequacy and powerlessness by developing an inflated sense of your own power and self-importance. I call this pseudo-independence.

> *'Pride goeth before destruction,*
> *and a haughty spirit before a fall.'*
> *– Bible, Proverbs 16:18*

Pseudo-Independence or False Pride

Pseudo-independence is basically false pride. It is the way you might cope with feelings of helplessness and shame, with feeling small, by denying those feelings, by putting up a false front. Paradoxically, this is also how you stop yourself from growing up. This kind of over-assertion of independence is reactionary and rebellious, which is common at adolescence, but it is not genuine separation. Although it looks like the polar opposite of dependency, the underlying feelings are similar. Some call this counter-dependency, which has the same cause as codependency.

If you are asserting your independence in this way, you are reacting *against* dependency, rather than growing out of it. If you do not have a strong sense of who you are, this can be your way of inventing yourself – a kind of façade. This façade is not your true identity. It can be proud and aloof. You pretend detachment when you have not separated completely, when you have not separated from your childhood needs, only denied them, and the pain of not having had them met; when you have not separated from parents whose recognition you needed and did not get. You need to drop your pretence and listen to yourself because you were not listened to as a child or adolescent.

False pride is also rigid, defensive, superior, competitive and controlling. This can be seen in the story of Rachel and Keith.

Rachel and Keith had been married for twenty-one years. Keith was prominent in politics. After she had children, Rachel became depressed and she stayed on medication for most of her marriage. Because Rachel did not have the confidence to pursue the career she had started after graduating, she chose to play a supporting role to Keith and his career, which she then resented. She also chose to look after the home and the children. Rachel wanted Keith to support her in this but she found, over the years, that he was emotionally detached, cold, patronising and often abusive if she spoke up, hitting her if he could not get his own way. Although Rachel coped well with her chosen role, she said she felt emotionally dependent on Keith, because of her depression. In fact, Keith's work caused him to travel frequently, usually without her, so he was not there very often for her to depend on anyway. Keith complained that Rachel had taken control of the home and children but he also used his career to excuse his unavailability. Rachel did, in fact, use controlling behaviour to compensate for her feelings of dependency, frequently making decisions about the home or the children without consulting Keith.

When their children were grown up, Rachel gradually reduced her medication and went back to work, gained more confidence and progressed quickly in her career as an administrator. She found she no longer needed Keith in the way she thought she did before. She refused to sleep with him, because of his abusiveness, and wanted to end the marriage. As a result of this Keith started drinking heavily and became more violent when Rachel challenged him. Rachel moved out of the family home. Keith spent long periods of time crying and begging her to come back, while still arguing with her and blaming her for the breakdown of the marriage. This caused his work to deteriorate. It became obvious, by that stage of their marriage, that he was far more dependent on her than she was on him.

Keith had not grown up. He was the baby in his family. His older sisters said his parents drank and fought with each other. At first, Keith did not remember this and said they were happy. We established that his basic dependency needs were not adequately met because his parents were too involved in their own problems to be available to him. Keith compensated by detaching emotionally, avoiding intimacy, and pretending not to need anybody. He also fought with his sisters during adolescence. He became ambitious in his career. His prominent role in society helped support his independent façade, which masked a great fear of being abandoned, plus denial of his dependency, to the extent that he could not accept that he had been rejected by Rachel and was now alone.

Keith had to face the fact that, in many ways, he was still immature. He was still craving the safety, containment and nurturing he did not have as a child and the recognition he did not get as an adolescent. In order to grow up, he had to admit his fear of abandonment and feelings of helplessness, inadequacy and rejection, comparing those childhood feelings to the reality of his present life and his childhood and adolescent needs to the reality of his adult needs. In this way he has been able to start separating from his past and moving towards true independence. Keith is struggling to live alone and become his own person, which he has never been before. He tells me it is a revelation to him that his pride has kept him cut off from so much that he could have had over the years of his marriage; so much he has gone without in his adult life. He tells me how exhausting it has been to keep up his façade of independence and how lonely and scared he has felt for so long, personally and professionally.

> *'There is no dependence that can be sure*
> *but a dependence upon one's self. '*
> *– John Gay*

Rachel and Keith Depended on One Another

During the course of his marriage, Keith's façade of independence *depended* on Rachel's dependency, and on the role he was playing. Rachel enabled him to be the 'man' and he enabled her to be the 'woman' in their family. When Rachel changed her role, Keith's independence fell apart. It was not based on inner security. He was attempting to get Rachel to meet his unmet childhood needs, and to make him feel like a man, but he was also alienating her. She no longer found it appropriate to parent a grown man, or to prop up his masculinity. During the marriage, Rachel, although feeling dependent on Keith, also got a sense of power and autonomy from the knowledge that Keith depended on her. She would often use this against him, which alienated him more. This was her false pride. She also believed she needed him emotionally when he had never supported her emotionally anyway.

Rachel took a submissive, dependent role, denying her independence and allowing Keith to be dominant. The illusion of his masculinity made her feel feminine, but also weak. She felt more comfortable in a supporting role. Dominance fulfilled Keith's emotional needs by giving him a sense of autonomy, authority and importance, as well as making him feel like a 'man'. It allowed him to deny his dependence. Rachel's supporting role meant she did not have to face taking responsibility in the world or in a career, which frightened her. Nor did she have to mature sexually and allow genuine intimacy. Her choice to stay home was not made from a position of true independence. Both Rachel and Keith were suffering from incomplete independence and immature sexuality. They were still clinging to unfulfilled childhood needs and adolescent competitiveness. Rachel was stronger emotionally and Keith was better able to make his way in the world. When Rachel reversed her role by attempting to fulfil her potential in the world, they were in trouble. Keith was then challenged to attend to his emotional development, his ability to be open and receptive to intimacy and to need people in relationships that did not have an inbuilt guarantee; that is: the dependence of the other person. However, dependency and pseudo-independence served Rachel and Keith for a long time, even though there was always a price to pay. For Rachel this was Keith's rejection of her and for Keith it was Rachel's sniping and nagging – another form of rejection.

> 'The hidden danger in having a separative outlook is that, while it appears to serve our best interests in the short run, it can eventually lead us into that dreaded and all-too-common ailment, loneliness.' – Alan Harris, Suicide and the Agony of Separateness: When the Ego Becomes an Eggshell

As you can see from Keith's story, false independence is as fragile as an eggshell, and ultimately very lonely. Rachel managed to achieve true independence when her dependency was no longer safe or comfortable for her; when she no longer found it attractive as a way of life, although I do not know what she did about maturing sexually. When Keith realised how much pain his false pride and pseudo-independent position had caused him, he took steps to change it.

If you are pseudo-independent, you will find it hard to ask for help. You have a fear of love and intimacy because it makes you feel needy, vulnerable and also open to rejection. Yet your false independence leaves you feeling cold and lonely, even if it does lead you to believe you are in control of your emotions; it helps you keep hidden what you feel is shameful or 'weak' about you, because it was once rejected, whether this was your neediness as a child, your sexuality as an adolescent or anything else that might make you feel vulnerable and requires trusting someone else.

Maturing Sexually

False pride is an ineffective strategy for dealing with the kind of rejection that can come from your parent of the opposite sex at adolescence; their failure to recognize you as a mature, sexual man or woman. Earlier, childhood rejection is more likely to cause dependent, rather than pseudo-independent, behaviour. You may use immature strategies, like trying to please, to gain acceptance, but this means regressing to 'little girl' or 'little boy'; it is not fulfilling. You pretend you do not care, but this kind of rejection hurts like hell because your love has been rejected along with your sexual maturity; so you end up pushing your partner away, (from your heart), and only *use* them for need-fulfilment rather than *sharing* the joys of mature love and sexuality expressed through genuine intimacy. You use your genitals to keep them away from your wounded heart. You do not become a mature man or woman because your heart is emotionally cold. This can cause sexual frigidity or promiscuous acting out. If you do not have a partner, or even if you do, you may unconsciously keep members of the opposite sex at arms length. If your parent of the same sex was jealous of you, you will be afraid to own your mature sexuality because you felt threatened by them.

For You to Think About:

How false pride prevents you from getting what you need as an adult.

> 'The pathos of man is that he hungers for personal fulfilment
> and for a sense of community with others.'
> – J. Saunders Redding

5

UP IS NOT A PLACE WHERE GROWING COMES TO AN END

> *'Imagine all the people sharing all the world.'*
> *Imagine – John Lennon 1971*

Interdependence – Sharing and Co-operation

Interdependence is about sharing and co-operation. Gaining independence is an important part of growing up. Then you can:

- safely allow other people into your life.
- relate with other independent people.
- share your gifts, talents and resources.
- ask for help and support.

Although you may enjoy periods of solitude, in the long term, you will almost certainly be lonely. As an adult, contact-seeking social and sexual creature, you do need other people, but not in the same way you did when you were a helpless child.

Interdependence is about all kinds of relationships. It describes how you interact and co-operate with other people. You do this in a variety of situations; in intimate, sexual, social, commercial and economic, mutually supportive relationships, families, communities and networks. In order to live the complex life that modern people have, you need other people to share and exchange with, in one way or another. However, you cannot share what you do not have. Interdependence is about independent people sharing. So you cannot inter-depend if you are not first independent. To the extent that you do not have your own integrity, you are less likely to act conscientiously toward others; and more likely to inter-relate with people who lack integrity. To the extent that you are still dependent, you are more likely to use people as need-fulfilling objects than to relate with them as people. You are also unlikely to co-operate if you are still in adolescent rebellion. Co-operation is an essential ingredient of maturity.

Where Do You Belong?

> '........ we are, each of us, necessarily social beings,
> individuals created through relationships with others'.
> – Patricia Hewitt

Participating in relationships, families, social and spiritual networks and communities, gives you a sense of belonging, which helps you affirm who you are, define yourself, feel rooted in your identity and connected to something bigger than you. This helps you to grow, emotionally and spiritually, and stimulates you intellectually. It gives meaning and context to your life. Belonging involves relationships with other people who have common goals, ideals, interests and causes, who are not necessarily your family. If they are healthy, these relationships are interdependent and allow you your independence. But, if these shared ideals are based on powerlessness, paranoia, helplessness and dependency, although they may give you a sense of belonging, these relationships do not help you to grow because they do not promote true independence; only a reactionary kind of pseudo-independence. They keep you dependent.

If your relationships are based on independence and autonomy, they help you to develop your potential, adding meaning to your life through shared and appropriate intimacy, (not to be confused with familiarity). Mutually you can help one another to become more of who you are.

> Interdependent relationships are fulfilling.
> This increases your sense of well being.

How Does Interdependence Differ From Dependence?

Interdependence is not the same as adult dependency. It differs from dependence because it is:

- Mature
- Equal

- Reciprocal
- Co-operative (but not collusive)
- An exchange, both giving and receiving
- Not mutually supportive of regressive, immature needs but;
- Effective in getting your adult needs met.

In fact, it is the only way to get your needs adequately met in an adult way.

You can choose whom you inter-depend with; but there is little element of choice in dependency, which is based on the belief that you have no other choice, when often you do.

In the more intimate of interdependent relationships, when you are truly independent, you can have a balance between stimulation, or challenge, and comfort. This is something near to dependability, or good enough security. Your relationships are more likely to be viable, effective and healthy. These kinds of relationships are likely to be stable enough to continue, but flexible enough to allow, enable, and facilitate growth and change. You can make mistakes, learn from them, be forgiven and progress in developing your potential.

> *'In love the paradox occurs that two beings become one
> and yet remain two.'
> – Erich Fromm*

In these relationships you bond with one another, but you do not merge. You have clear and separate identities and personal boundaries. You do not lose your independence; you share it. Because you have your own personal autonomy, you do not attempt to control each other. Nor do you make immature and unrealistic demands on one another. You are able to love one another.

> *Interdependence is not an alternative
> to independence.*

Mature Love Comes from Loving Yourself

I believe that love based on dependency is not love, but need. It is an attempt to possess the other person so they will fulfil your perceived needs. Mature love is based on interdependence. In mature love:

- You love yourself.
- You are not dependent on another person for love.
- You feel separate from them.
- Yet you are able to allow intimacy, without losing your identity.
- You love them for who they are, not for what they can do for you.
- Your love is unconditional (but see below).
- You are prepared to let them go if that is what they need to do.
- You never stop loving them, even if you choose to separate.
- You care about their well-being, but do not attempt to rescue them from their own responsibility.
- You feel richer when you are in their company, because you like them and because you like yourself the way you are when you are with them.
- But you are not dependent on them for this 'good' feeling.
- You already feel good in yourself.
- You have no need to cling to them.
- You are healthily attached; you can detach, but are not aloof.
- You have no need to comply with them or attempt to control them.

Mature love is the same whether there is sexual desire or not; and it is the same love you feel for children as you feel for adults, of both sexes.

Unconditional Love:
It is possible to reject behaviours without rejecting people,
if you find those behaviours unacceptable.

Interdependent relationship may present challenges. If your love is mature you accept these challenges, as well as feeling safe to challenge too. You are not afraid to assert yourself when necessary. You allow change to happen in your relationships. You address conflict when it arises.

Desmond and Sandra's Story

Desmond and Sandra are some people I know whose relationship is an example of mature love.

> Desmond and Sandra were friends for some years. They eventually became a couple. They loved one another and had a healthy, mature relationship. They were both studying and planned to marry when they finished. However, unexpected events in both their lives meant they had to part. The love between them had not changed, only the nature of their relationship. They are no longer a couple, but their love is not dependent on this.
> However, their relationship has not been without conflict.

Conflict Helps You Grow

In life, with all its paradoxes, uncertainty and changes, conflict is inevitable. In dependent relationships compliance and controlling ensure that conflict is mostly denied because it upsets the status quo. How you acknowledge and manage conflict is important, particularly in terms of pain reduction and conservation of valuable emotional energy. You can welcome conflict as a challenge. You can use it constructively, rather than destructively. It is an opportunity for change. Conflict, and learning how to resolve it, helps you to grow and to mature. You will feel better after it is resolved than you did before it arose.

You are likely to experience conflict at times of change and transition, when you have to make decisions that are often extremely difficult and to learn new ways of being. You may struggle with letting go of what served you in the past, even though it is not what is required now. You may also need to grieve for what is passing. Conflict is a by-product of growth, a breaking down of equilibrium. It is a temporary loss of balance while a new state of balance is forming.

In the absence of effective strategies for conflict resolution within yourself, or in your relationships, stress may cause you to regress to stages of your childhood or adolescence where conflict was not resolved. You may act out original struggles, with yourself or your parents, with anyone else you are in relationship with. You are likely to resort to the coping behaviours you used then. Although these helped you survive, they did not resolve your conflict then. They do not resolve either your present or your past conflict now. They usually add to it, confuse you and increase and prolong your pain. To avoid this pain you may resort to denial or blaming. This keeps you trapped in unresolved conflicts from the past that continue to colour your present and prevent you from progressing and developing.

It is only when you stop blaming that you learn to face and identify inner conflicts that are triggered by external conflicts. You can do this by checking out whether you are *responding* as an adult or *reacting* as a child, driven by emotions you could not manage in the past and are trying to avoid now. By allowing these emotions now, you can also face your fears and bring them into perspective. Then you are able to take responsibility for the decisions you are making in the present.

> *'Underground issues from one relationship or context invariably fuel our fires in another.'*
> *– Harriet Lerner*

It Was Like This for Sandra and Desmond

When the time came for them to make career decisions, Desmond's choices were not compatible with Sandra's. Sandra found she had to move some four hundred miles away, which she had not expected. Desmond was unable to join her, having received an opportunity he had not planned for and could not turn down because of sudden family commitments. Both of their lives had changed.

In their distress at being separated, Sandra accused Desmond of being weak and abandoning her and Desmond became aloof and withdrew, refusing to answer her letters and telephone calls. Sandra deflected her pain by attacking and blaming Desmond. She knew she could not be part of Desmond's new life and also be true to herself, so she tried to reject him completely, sending back the books and gifts he had given her. She also wrote long letters demanding that he pay attention to her grief.

Desmond did not know how to do this. He felt guilty. He could do nothing to change the situation so he ignored Sandra completely. He deflected his pain by avoiding the conflict. It was too distressing for him to be in contact with her at that time.

Under stress, they both regressed to the dependent, immature and ineffective behaviours they had learned as coping strategies when they were in conflict as children. This was an attempt to have some control over the situation. They coped with their conflicting needs to be separate and make independent decisions, and also the resulting feelings of abandonment and loss, as they had done then. They abandoned one another. This did not resolve anything and they lost contact for a whole year.

Then, by chance, they came into contact again. Time had healed their pain enough for them to discuss what happened, and why. They have acknowledged and accepted the difference in their life paths and life styles. They have been able to continue their friendship and the mutual support they used to give one another. They have taken responsibility for the independent choices they made. They still love each other dearly and have forgiven each other for behaving badly, and immaturely, under stress.

Sandra and Desmond have learned that changes need not mean endings; and that separation need not mean abandonment, although they have realised it felt like that for both of them as children. They have retrieved what is valuable and interdependent in their relationship and let go of what is no longer workable – being a couple. They have accepted their disappointments. Although they both experienced pain and conflict, they have grown through this and learned to love each other without expectations. Both of them say they feel stronger and more self-confident for having done this.

'O God, give us serenity to accept what cannot be changed,
and courage to change what would be changed,
and wisdom to distinguish the one from the other.'
– Dr. Reinhold Niebuhr

For You to Think About:

Your own support systems.
What love is based on for you.

'No man is an island, entire of itself;
every man is a piece of the continent, a part of the main.'
– John Donne

Part II

Using What You've Got

6

RESPONSIBILITY NEED NOT BE A BURDEN

'In the long run, we shape our lives, and we shape ourselves.
The process never ends until we die.
And the choices we make are ultimately our own responsibility.'
– Eleanor Roosevelt

The Benefits of Growing Up

Your life is a continuous work in progress. You grow over time. You do not always complete stages of your growth at the age when it might be most suitable. You can catch up at any time. You experience the benefits of growing up gradually. You experience them when you are little as you are able and as your parents and your environment provide the opportunities. You become more capable of taking on responsibility for yourself as you get older. Your gradual experience accumulates, until you are an adult, when you are able to take over the responsibility for yourself from your parents. Then there are still more experiences; there is more growing up to do; there are more benefits to have. You can choose, and have an effect on, your environment. You can, if you wish, continue to seek opportunities for growing.

Responsibility and Freedom

The ability to take responsibility is a gift because it gives you freedom from dependency.

'Although you may not always be able to avoid difficult situations,
you can modify the extent to which you suffer
by how you choose to respond to the situation.'
– H H The Dalai Lama

Responsibility is the willingness and the ability to be answerable, to respond to the choices available to you and then to stand by your decisions and act on them.

There is a difference between responding and reacting. When you respond you deal with situations in an appropriate, realistic and satisfying manner, adapting to them by making choices. When you react, you are fighting against situations, pushing them away and denying yourself the possibility of having choices, and therefore freedom. You are acting out your emotions, as a child might, without thinking about the effect of your actions, or the consequences. This is not satisfying, although it may be comforting for a while. When you respond, you are accepting your situation and considering how to deal with it before acting. Thus responsibility, or response-ability, requires careful thought, and maturity.

Unfortunately, responsibility has been associated with other words like liability, duty and obligation. In this way guilt has have been attached to responsibility; something you think you ought, must, should do, not that you want to do. This implies there is no choice available. Responsibility is always a choice, just as *not* taking responsibility is a choice, both with their own consequences.

I suggest you try removing the words 'should', 'must' and 'ought' from your vocabulary. Try finding alternatives that empower you, like 'I want to', 'I feel the need to' or 'I believe it would be good for me to.' Ask yourself, 'Who says I ought, must, should?' Nobody has the right to tell you this now. Think about whose voice is directing your decisions. Whose voice is still making you feel guilty?

> *'If you take responsibility for yourself*
> *you will develop a hunger to accomplish your dreams.'*
> *– Les Brown*

Although I believe that the ability to take responsibility brings you freedom, responsibility has also been associated with burden. I do not see that freedom can ever be a burden, even though it can cause anxiety, if you are not used to it, not prepared for it or do not know how to manage it. However, if you take on too much responsibility, you are likely to feel overwhelmed by it. You need to know your own limitations. Taking on responsibility frequently means taking on work, so you may have to work for the freedom it brings. Creative and purposeful work done willingly and without resentment ultimately frees you because it improves your life, fulfils your potential and brings you a sense of achievement and pleasure. You also achieve the gift of learning, practising and perfecting skills, which increases your resourcefulness, confidence and self-esteem; you feel more capable. The responsibility you take on helps you fulfil your dreams.

Taking responsibility means moving from childhood to maturity, from comfort to pleasure, a process that I explained earlier. This is what moves you from the limitations of childhood to the freedom of maturity. Any responsibility that does not do this may feel like a burden and you may have to think about making changes that do free you. It is possible to give up responsibilities that you have taken on if they become unproductive and unduly burdensome. That is why, to the best of your ability, you need to be informed before you make choices and decisions. There is a difference between responsibility that frees you and burdens that trap you.

Freedom and Choice

> 'The strongest principle of growth lies in human choice.'
> – George Eliot

I have said that independence brings you freedom. The more independent you become, the more choices you have. To exercise choice you need to make decisions and then take responsibility for having made them. Taking responsibility for your decisions is using your autonomy. This gives you freedom, even if this freedom is limited to the choices available to you at any time, (or the choices you believe are available). As you grow out of helplessness and dependency, you become aware of more and more choices you can have. I frequently discover there are choices I never knew I could have and therefore my life becomes even richer than I thought it could be.

Here is an exercise for you:

- When you feel burdened by the responsibilities you have taken on, ask yourself what you really want most.
- How would you really like your life to be, realistically?
- Then ask yourself how you might go about having that.
- What choices are available to you, and are there more than that? Do some research.
- The important question is then, what would you have to give up in order to move from where you are now to where you want to be?
- What are you ready to give up now?
- What can you see yourself giving up in the future, and when?
- You may well find, when you ask yourself whether you really want these things any more anyway, you do not, because where you want to move to is so much more suited to your needs.
- Remember false pride. Would you have to let that go?
- Then you can see how you are trapping yourself.
- You might also ask yourself what purpose this burdensome responsibility has served. (Remember false pride again).
- If that purpose is outlived, then it is time to give yourself permission to move on.
- This may take some time, but possibly less than you think it will once you have made your mind up.

Your choices may be about what someone else wants you to do or about what you want to do yourself. In making decisions on choices available, you learn to consider consequences and outcomes. You may also choose to make joint decisions in interdependent relationships, in which case there is shared as well as personal responsibility. Decision making requires the gathering of information.

> *'Liberty means responsibility.*
> *That is why most men dread it.'*
> *– George Bernard Shaw*

Liberty may mean responsibility, but responsibility also means liberty. Liberty means free will. You might not want liberty if you feel insecure and are clinging to comfort and familiarity or if you do not feel capable and are afraid of having to work for the benefits of responsibility and freedom. If this is so for you, as I suggested in Chapter 1, you might want to look at the pain you are trying to comfort, that is holding you back from working and being creative. There may have been a time in the past when your will was thwarted, your freedom was restricted, or your hopes and dreams were crushed or stolen, which was painful. Or perhaps you were mature enough to make your own decisions and were not allowed to. Perhaps you had to comply with the wishes of other people who had power or control over you. Perhaps you did not know what options were available to you. But this is probably not how it is now. It may be that you had to take on too much responsibility too soon, when you were not emotionally equipped to, which leaves you resenting and avoiding responsibility now. Pain from the past can become a burden that is trapping you in the present. You can move through that pain by acknowledging it, offloading that burden and then move on in the present. You will find you do not need that pain any more, you do not need to suffer because your life has changed as you have matured; you have other choices now.

You might also want to look at your insecurity and how you approach risk taking. If you are clinging to irresponsibility, it may be you are stuck in rebellion, angry, and need to use your anger creatively. You may be afraid of not knowing *how* to do what you want to do, but you can always *learn* how.

Taking on responsibility that is not your own burdens you. If you take away the responsibility of another person, you deprive them of the benefit of their own experience. This does not allow them to grow; therefore it traps them in dependency. This is not the same as sharing responsibility or interdepending.

> 'The outward freedom that we shall attain
> will only be in exact proportion to the inward freedom
> to which we may have grown at a given moment.'
> – Mahatma Gandhi

Because responsibility means you are accountable, it is also related to issues of trust. If you take responsibility for your decisions, then it follows you are acting with integrity. If you act with integrity, you are trustworthy. Your ability to take responsibility depends on how far you have grown out of dependency and into your autonomy and therefore integrity. Freedom is within you. You may well find it is *you* who is holding you back. Your outward freedom will be matched by your inner freedom as you make changes in your life that reflect your degree of maturity and as you learn to give yourself **ENCOURAGEMENT** and **PERMISSION** – and also allow yourself to mess up occasionally.

In my experience, opportunities always exist, especially when you dare to widen your expectations and open your mind to more diverse possibilities than those you have learned to expect. It is your choice whether you take them up or not.

Blaming or Apportioning Responsibility

> *'The reason people blame things on previous generations is that there's only one other choice.'*
> *– Doug Larson*

We are fond of blaming. We say something is someone's *fault*. I do not find blaming constructive. I find it much more helpful to be able to think in terms of responsibility. When you were a child your parents were responsible for you to the extent that you were not able to be responsible for yourself. They were also responsible for their actions, as were other adults in your life. You were never responsible for adults or their actions, even though you may have blamed yourself. In the absence of any other explanation, children do blame themselves. It also follows that, if you hold yourself responsible for the actions of someone else, you are assuming a greater power than you really have. This is misleading and distorted thinking.

As an adult, you are responsible for yourself, whether you like it or not. You are responsible for your actions and for dealing with your feelings, even when those feelings are triggered by someone else's actions. Blaming someone or something else will not change this. You cannot change the past, so you have no other choice but to make changes in the present, regardless of the circumstances of, or the mistakes your parents made in, your upbringing – or the choices *you* made at that time. Only you are responsible for your present. If you do not like someone else's behaviour, you usually have choices. You also have the power of articulation. You can communicate how you feel without blaming someone else.

If you hold someone else responsible for your present life, feelings or actions, you are giving power to that person and depleting your own. You are putting yourself in the position of victim, which means keeping yourself helpless and immature, when you are not. You are limiting your own freedom. You are less likely to change anything if you are blaming someone else. By taking responsibility for your life now, you are likely to feel more capable and mature; and to gain self-respect and self-esteem. Blaming does not increase self-esteem, only competitiveness and conflict. It is a means of deflecting your feelings, instead of feeling them, owning them and communicating. Blaming is a form of denial.

However, you are entitled to feel angry about things that happened to you in the past. The potent way to deal with this anger is to apportion responsibility more realistically and hand it back to where it belongs, actually or symbolically. Handing back responsibility to others, with whom it more appropriately belongs, does not mean you need not take responsibility for yourself in the present.

A Short Story

> Maya's father was a domineering man. Her mother chose to comply with his wishes, rather than incur the ugly scenes he made if he did not get his own way. They came to stay with Maya for the weekend. Her father wanted to watch an important tennis match on the television and her mother wanted to go shopping in the town, so Maya drove her. They arranged to meet up at Maya's house when the match ended and go out to dinner.

Maya noticed that her mother was not comfortable when they were shopping. She was very nervous about getting back to her husband on time. But she was also enjoying her time alone with her daughter. Because of this, Maya did not take seriously several reminders her mother gave her about the time. Nor did her mother insist they leave. When they arrived back at Maya's house, fifteen minutes after the match ended, her father had left. Her mother was hurt and distressed. Maya and her mother went to the restaurant they had talked about with her father, but he was not there. He eventually turned up at Maya's house, having had dinner with another relative.

Maya told me she was very upset to see her mother so hurt. She felt responsible for what had happened. But she also felt angry. We talked about the apportionment of responsibility. I suggested that she was taking on too much of it.

Maya felt genuinely sorry for not having listened to her mother's concern about the time, because she, too, was enjoying their time together. She also resented her mother's fear of her father. But she realised it had been her mother's responsibility to make her wishes clear about being taken back to meet her husband. She also understood it was her mother's responsibility to deal with the fear and pain her husband's behaviour caused her. Maya learned that she was not responsible for the behaviour of her father or her mother, nor for the decisions they had made in their relationship with one another.

Having symbolically handed back this responsibility to those it belonged with, Maya was able to detach from the situation and feel less angry. She agreed that her mother is a grown woman, able to take responsibility for herself, and, although it feels hard for her, she realises she can do nothing to rescue her from the situation she has chosen to live in.

For You to Think About:

How you apportion responsibility in your life.

> 'The most important persuasion tool you have
> in your entire arsenal
> is integrity.'
> – Zig Ziglar

7

ON THE BEST AUTHORITY

> *'This above all; to thine own self be true.'*
> *– William Shakespeare*

Integrity

One of the joys of growing up is having integrity. This means being true to yourself and not compromising who you are; also using and being true to your own conscience and not breaking your own rules. This is not the same as feeling guilty or being afraid to break someone else's rules, which may not necessarily be right for you, in line with your own conscience or reflect your truth. But you do need to observe the rules of the land you live in, even if you do not agree with them or they are limiting, because you are aware of the consequences of breaking them. It is also about treating other people as you would like to be treated yourself.

You feel complete, whole and healthy when you live according to your own conscience because you are living your truth. You feel at home and at one with yourself. And you value yourself for who you are by being it. You have the freedom of being your own person. This has an effect on other people. They feel able to trust you because you are genuine; integrity does not need façades. You also feel moral without being self-righteous because you are acting with autonomy, not arrogance. Integrity and independence are closely related because it is hard to have integrity as an adult if you are still dependent and compromising your true self.

Your own morality brings satisfaction, rather than comfort; it gives you inner security, because you are not split, not pulled between someone else's reality and your own. You feel more solid and centred within yourself. Those times of struggle, uncertainty and changes feel worthwhile because they increase your integrity. In these transitions you become more of who you are, more independent, more self-reliant and therefore freer, even though a part of you may break down and even dissolve away in the process;

this is the process of healing yourself, becoming more whole. What you lose is usually not part of your integrity, but part of the defence you have built up to use instead. You build up defences to hold yourself together when you do not feel whole, when you are not integrated.

You may also have to sacrifice dependency to have integrity. Nevertheless, there may be times when you compromise in order to have dependency, or to survive in circumstances that are not best for you.

> 'That you may retain your self-respect,
> it is better to displease the people by doing what you know is right,
> than to temporarily please them by doing what you know is wrong.'
> – William J. H. Boetcker

Inner and Outer Authority

As you grow in integrity, you gain authority, which means knowing yourself and knowing what is right and wrong *for you*. Nobody else can know this. True authority springs from being your own person, being whole and allowing yourself to be who you are. It is your truth, what you experience and what you feel. Nobody else can have your experience for you. Only you know what you feel, even if others may be able to empathise. And what you feel is true for you. It is *your* authority about *you*. If you deny what you feel to please or comply, you compromise your integrity. You are less believable, because, after all, you are not being honest. If you are not believable, you do not have authority. So, owning what you know, even if it is only about you, gives you integrity. Authority and integrity grow together.

If you have true, inner authority, you know what your rights are, because you know what is right for you; then you can exercise free will and genuinely take responsibility. You also know when your rights are being abused.

Many of you grew up with models of authority that deny what you feel. You may have been taught that other people, those 'in authority', knew better than you. These people, because they denied your reality, which you may also have learned to deny, had authority *over* you. This is not authority, it is bullying.

> 'Unthinking respect for authority
> is the greatest enemy of truth.'
> – Albert Einstein

You may also have learned to understand authority as a given role, a vested right. Any vested right that denies your rights is not true authority. Being in a position of authority is not necessarily proof that you have any, although you would hope that those with authority are put in these positions. Authority may be 'given' to those with greater seniority or even the ability to exercise power *over* other people, to exact obedience, usually by fear or force or dependency. Many of you will have been taught to 'look up' to these people without questioning them. True authority is not frightening or punishing, although it may make boundaries. These are models of exterior authority and authority *over*. True, inner authority comes from learning and experience. So beware of people *in* authority who do not, in fact, *have* any, or those who claim to have it when they have none. Remember to check out your own because you know what is right for you.

Geraldine's Story

Geraldine had two lively children, a boy of eleven and a girl of twelve. She worked from home making curtains. Her husband worked in a factory and came home late. He ate his meal alone in front of the television and then fell asleep.

Geraldine's policy was to allow the children to take a snack when they came home from school at four o'clock and to stop work herself at six o'clock, when she would prepare the evening meal and eat with the children. During those two hours they were rowdy and disturbing and she was in constant conflict with them. She would try to control them by making them sit in front of the television or go to their separate rooms to play. They rebelled and she spent more time during those hours trying to get them under control than she did working. When things got out of hand, the children would benefit from the sharp and hurtful edge of her tongue. They were rapidly learning to answer her back.

When Geraldine was at the end of her tether, she would call on her husband's authority. Her favourite saying was, 'Wait until your father gets home.' It was enough that the children knew he had a raging temper, (they had heard him use it on her), to subdue them. Geraldine used his 'authority', which was really his raging and impotent anger, to threaten her children. It worked. 'You listen to your mother,' he would say, before sinking into what was known as 'your father's chair,' thus giving authority over the children to their mother. Geraldine talked about her husband as 'The man of the house,' and 'the head of the family.' She saw him as the ultimate authority. She did nothing to take up her own. She also told me that, in her childhood, her own father's word was law. 'He only had to raise his voice,' she said. Her mother's role had been to look after the home and children.

Geraldine believed her children did not respect her because she was weak, but did respect their father because he was strong. She complained of not being able to control them. She also complained about her husband's violent temper.

In therapy Geraldine and I examined her ideas of male and female roles within a family. We looked at what authority really is. She began to see that her father had no real authority in her family; he controlled his children through fear, but he did not know them and was never close to them. This was also true of her husband. She saw that his authority was dependent on his being the 'nominal' head of the family, a position she gave to him, although she was actually running it. Geraldine saw how powerful her own mother really was, because she was looking after her family's *and* her husband's needs, although she was not owning that power but giving it to her husband. We began to look at how Geraldine could use her own power more effectively to take control of, rather than trying to control, her children and to change her relationship with her husband.

Like true morality, true authority is humble. Authority is something you will *feel,* if you own it. You will be able to admit what you know and what you do not.

Knowledge, Experience and Expertise

> 'The only real security that a man will have in this world is a reserve of knowledge, experience, and ability.'
> – Henry Ford

Knowledge, experience and expertise are important assets acquired over time.

In order to know what you are talking about, and to make informed choices, you need knowledge, which comes from gathering information and gaining experience. It also comes through education, through encouraging, developing, cultivating and bringing out your innate capacities which, hopefully, your education did for you and which you can continue to do as an adult.

You gain experience and learn as you grow. Some of this experience comes from making mistakes. You will not want to try new experiences if you have been punished or humiliated for making mistakes. If you have been forced to accept the authority of your parents and teachers, rather than being allowed to learn through experiencing for yourself, you will be using their authority and not your own. At best this is based on their experience, not yours. Beware of using second-hand authority. It is not genuine. Check out what *you* feel, what *you* believe and what *you* know.

You gain skills as you grow up. As you learn and practise skills, you gain expertise and ability; you grow confident and learn to believe in yourself. Knowledge, experience and expertise increase your authority. Because you learn through experience, you also learn from the models you experienced in your childhood. These models were not always right for you. Like Geraldine, you may need to question them and find effective models for yourself. You may need to question what you accepted as authority.

Knowledge gives you power. But, if your knowledge is not used with integrity, it can be dangerous and manipulative. Likewise, you may have integrity, but, if you do not have knowledge, although you may have inner authority, it will not be effective. You need at least to know how to speak your truth. Many people grow up without the skill of articulating how they feel. Many do not know the difference between feelings and thoughts.

When you say something like, 'I feel you're angry with me,' what do you really mean? I think either you mean, 'I *feel* threatened by you,' or, 'I *think* you are angry with me.'

When you say, 'You make me feel angry,' I think you really mean, 'I feel angry when you do that.' This means admitting what you feel, your experience of you, rather than blaming the other person.

Articulation is an essential gift of maturity, a valuable skill worth developing. You will find it an invaluable tool for getting you out of many scrapes and tight corners, as well as for resolving interpersonal conflicts.

Many people also grow up not knowing they have the ability to think as well as feel. Children sometimes make what sound like insightful and logical statements. This is because they see the truth without embellishment or the denial they may later be taught or learn. They use their innate wisdom, but without using logic or reason, which are gifts you develop as you grow up and abilities you do not have as a small child. Logic and reason help you to utilise your innate wisdom. Many adults forget to use these gifts. They do not think before they act or consider the consequences of their actions. Many adults also deny their innate wisdom. If you can apply logic and reason to inner wisdom, you have true authority. But beware you neither analyse your feelings away nor that your logic becomes illogical because you are using it to deny what you feel. If you use logic and reason to deny your experience and your reality, you have no authority.

Power and Control

As you grow into and take up your authority, slowly, over time, and at various stages of your life, you take up your personal power. Your power comes from living your truth – your integrity and your authority.

> *'The less people know about what is really going on, the easier it is to wield power and authority.'*
> *– Charles, Prince of Wales*

Knowledge and information are powerful. They free you from ignorance and enable you to act. They let you assess where you stand and what your options are. Therefore, a good way of controlling people is to deprive them of information. Think about secrets in your family and what information was withheld from you. Think about your own denial or compromising. This is a way of keeping information, your truth, from yourself. You can also think about what information was not available to you, simply because your parents, or teachers, did not know where to find it either. So many times people tell me they thought the behaviour in their family normal and right because they had no other information or experience of families who behaved differently.

However much power you have, it is your own, personal power. It feels good to experience this power. This good feeling is not at the expense of anyone else. You are not taking anything away from them, using them or depending on anyone else for this feeling. You are independent. Nor do you have power *over* anyone else, unless they choose to give you that power, (and you choose to take it). It follows that you, too, can give your power away to other people and then believe they have power *over* you. We often associate power with money, or even violence, frequently with superior physical strength, anything that can engender fear, intimidation or dependency.

> *'Power is a very gentle thing.'*
> *– Sun Bear*

True power is not frightening. It is pleasant to be around truly powerful people. When you have personal power, you do not feel a need to have power over other people, to control them, to have authority *over* them. You do not need to prove your power; it just is. You feel it inside you. When you think someone has power over you, think about how you are giving that power to them. One way is by abdicating from responsibility and becoming a victim, by letting them make choices for you. Another is by not taking up your own authority, or acting with integrity, particularly when you feel intimidated by them.

If you are afraid of authority in other people either:

- They do not have authority.
- You are not taking up your own authority.
- They are bullying you.
- You believe you are dependent on them.

As Geraldine's story illustrates, a difference exists between controlling, whether that is in your own life or trying to control someone else, and *taking* control. If you are controlling in your own life, you are not allowing yourself the flexibility and the freedom to grow. If you do not *take* control of your life, you are not taking responsibility for it and you will become a victim of circumstances instead. Your life will be unfocused, chaotic and probably less productive than it could be. This also applies to taking control of your children, (not the same as controlling them), while you are still responsible for them and while they are still unable to take control of themselves. If you do not do this, they will run your life and not learn to run their own. In either case you will have no freedom. So controlling and freedom do not go together, whether it is you or someone else who is doing it to you; but taking control, that is, making boundaries and decisions, and freedom, do. If you feel threatened, out of control, or that someone else is controlling you and you are dependent on them, you learn to use controlling as a defence. When your childhood is chaotic, you become controlling as a means of coping. Taking control is a more mature strategy for growing up and for helping your children grow up. It is a better way of being 'in control.'

The opposite of power is impotence. You may feel impotent when you are not equipped for situations that you encounter. You were impotent as a child to the extent that your physical, emotional, intellectual and spiritual resources were not yet developed. You may have continued to feel impotent if you were not helped, encouraged and allowed to develop these resources. As an adult you now have most of these resources available to you, or the ability to develop them as you choose.

You may be unclear about the extent of your own, personal power. You may believe you are omnipotent, because you were given too much power as a child and did not learn about discipline and the consequences of your actions. However, underneath this belief will be a feeling of powerlessness and insecurity. If this is true for you, as it was for Geraldine's husband, it is important to carefully and realistically assess the true extent of your authority, experience, power and integrity and to take measures to redress the balance and fill in the gaps. This is a way of taking control of your life now instead of hiding from it behind the façade of a power that is empty.

For You to Think About:

How you give power, control and authority to other people, who, and why.

Does your sense of power come from integrity or is it dependent on someone else?

> *'Respect your efforts, respect yourself.*
> *Self-respect leads to self-discipline.*
> *When you have both firmly under your belt, that's real power.'*
> *– Clint Eastwood*

8

MAKING LOVING DECISIONS

> *'The most assiduous task of parenting*
> *is to divine the difference between boundaries and bondage.'*
> – Barbara Kingsolver

What Are Boundaries?

Boundaries are limitations, rules; they are not barriers or bondage. Rules and limitations that are flexible and allow for change are joys of growing up. They promote a greater sense of well being and help you feel good about yourself. You gain respect when you make boundaries.

As you grow up, you learn to make boundaries in order to assert your autonomy, your ability to act and make decisions. You take responsibility, maintain and protect your integrity and take up your authority by making boundaries. You develop the free will and independence to be able to do this. You can use boundaries to discriminate by making choices, rather than incriminate by blaming. You learn how to do this from the way your parents and carers made boundaries for you.

Boundaries are not restrictions; they are healthy limitations. They are a way of organising your life. They are like a semi-permeable membrane that filters out what you do not want to take in and withholds what you do not want to put out. Making boundaries is a conscious choice. Healthy boundaries are flexible; they can expand and contract as you judge to be appropriate. Judgement is a gift of maturity. You learn it as your senses, experience and abilities develop and, as they do, you can manage wider and wider boundaries, you can allow more into your life and give out more of yourself and still feel safe. Making judgements is as different from *being* judgemental as taking control is from *being* controlling. You are more likely to be judgemental if you have not learned to make judgements and to assert your choices through discriminating and making boundaries as a means of securing your own safety.

Making appropriate boundaries is a skill that you can acquire. It takes practice and discipline to make clear, positive, affirmative statements and experience to know when you need to make them.

Protection and Defence

There is a difference between gentle boundaries that protect and defences, which are hostile barriers that wall you in. When you are defensive, you are behaving as if you are under siege. In most circumstances this is a reaction, rather than an appropriate response to what is needed. You have no filter or discrimination; nothing can get out, hence you have no means of creative expression, and nothing can get in, hence you get no nourishment. You close yourself off from any help and support, from communication and relationship. You may successfully wall out what you do not want, as long as you can manage to stay on the defensive, which takes a lot of energy, but you will also deprive yourself of what you do want and need.

If you are defensive, you cannot allow beginnings and endings, which need boundaries. So you prevent changes from happening and reduce your opportunities. You attempt to control through defensiveness, rather than taking control by making boundaries. If you are on the defensive, because you have no boundaries and therefore feel unsafe, you do not trust yourself or other people, which hostility increases your feelings of alienation, isolation and insecurity. If you know how to make boundaries, you trust your ability to take care of yourself in most situations. So, defences give an illusion of safety and security that is not safe at all; this fragile illusion depends on your belief that you have control. Such a defence is in fact a prison; it is a struggle; it is dependent on you having power over what you think is threatening you. It also demands a high degree of vigilance, which is exhausting.

What Do Boundaries Do?

> *When I feel angry*
> *I need to make a boundary.*

Boundaries protect you from external dangers, from violation, invasion, from being abused and victimised. They protect your rights. As a child, they protect your vulnerability, which, as an adult, becomes your sensitivity. If you do not know how to make boundaries, you will not be able to use this sensitivity, which is a gift. It needs protecting. Boundaries give you safety, but also freedom. They also enable you to take responsibility for yourself. There is no freedom without boundaries, because you are constantly fearful and anxious. In the extreme you will become hyper-vigilant, looking over your shoulder all the time and jumping at every slight or sound. But, boundaries separate and not everyone wants to be separate. If, as an adult, you are in a dependent relationship, you will not want to make boundaries. You will want to comply and compromise yourself, to merge with the other person, to feel like you are one person. But you will also remain a victim.

Boundaries contain, they do not control. Healthy parents use boundaries to contain their children. If you are a dependent adult, you may prefer to attempt control than to take the responsibility for making clear boundaries that also separate you and give you independence because you fear separation. As you are growing up, boundaries allow you gradual growth and expansion. Your parents make healthy boundaries that are appropriate to your age and abilities; boundaries that keep you safe but not restricted and teach you the extent of your own power and abilities. They give you consistency and stability and help to support and maintain your integrity. In this way you learn where you end and others begin.

Defining Yourself

So boundaries help you to define who you are, where you stand, what you want and what you do not want, without blame, shame or guilt because these are all things you have a right to do. You can also let other people know where they stand with you, without pushing them away. You can define and protect, not defend, your personal space. This promotes trust and intimacy, where it is appropriate. Your relationships are healthy. By defining yourself in this way you have a clear sense of your self and your rights; you validate yourself and your own reality. You gain self-respect and self-esteem. Other people respect you when you make boundaries. When you know you are able to protect yourself but also relate with other people, you feel safe and capable. However, this also means allowing other people to define their boundaries.

From Authoritarianism to Permissiveness

> 'The word "no" carries a lot more meaning
> when spoken by a parent
> who also knows how to say yes.'
> – Joyce Maynard

If your boundaries are too restrictive, you are able to do little more than survive. You are not able to really live. If you were controlled, rather than contained, as a child, you were brought up with rigid boundaries that were authoritarian and oppressive and have probably become overly controlled and controlling. If your parents were in possession of their own authority and using it, they would have made authoritative boundaries, based on their experience and expertise, rather than authoritarian, controlling boundaries that were too tight for you and prevented you from growing. If this is true for you, you may have thought you respected your parents, as Geraldine did, but you probably feared them, which is not the same. The paradox is, it was fear that made your parents controlling.

Inflexible boundaries suppress and frustrate. They are made in families that have a high level of compliant and controlling behaviour. Eventually they lead to explosion, where you turn your anger outwards as violence and rebellion; or implosion, where you turn you anger and frustration on yourself and become self-destructive, a victim. Restrictive boundaries do not engender respect, but fear; they are abusive and also motivated by fear.

Permissiveness is the path of least resistance and is equally as harmful, because, without boundaries that hold you, you are not safe. If your parents could not take up their responsibility to make boundaries for you, they did not protect you and you will not know how to protect yourself. You will not know how to grow up and will not have learned how to respect them, so you are less likely to respect yourself, your boundaries, or other people's. You may find your life overwhelming and chaotic and will find it difficult to organise yourself; and may also find it hard to express your creativity in a focused or constructive way.

> *You will always have to deal with what you postpone.*

Some parents are controlling and authoritarian until they run out of the energy and perseverance needed to control and then become permissive until they can no longer cope with the resulting chaos, when they revert to authoritarianism. They alternate between the two, but they never make clear and well defined boundaries. They either control or they comply. If your parents were like this, you probably grew up without respecting them, although you may have feared them, and not respecting yourself. This is how it was for Geraldine.

With tight boundaries, and with loose boundaries, you feel impotent, unsafe, defensive and incapable. You remain dependent.

Grey Areas

Boundaries are not always black or white. At times it may be difficult to make clear boundaries. You may feel torn between choices. One way to deal with grey areas is first to accept that you may not be ready to make a choice. You may need to 'feel' your way into what is right for you, or wait for these feelings to come. You may have got yourself into an unclear situation and are now finding it hard to extricate yourself. In the first instance, it helps to clarify what you want. You may think you 'should', 'must' or 'ought to' do something else. Ask yourself who said so. You will find that, when you let go of other people's judgement of you and what is right for you, you will be able to use your own judgement. You also need to look at what you have invested in being judged by other people. This may mean you do not have to take responsibility or assert your individuality. Maybe you want them to like and approve of you. Do you need this? Would you prefer to like yourself? Try to simplify. Stay with what you want. You will find that what was unclear and foggy becomes much clearer and simpler in time. You often get into grey areas when it is time for change and you are unaware you need to let go of something that has probably been serving your defensiveness, your false pride; something you no longer need and that is impeding your growth. Then you know it is time to make a new boundary to encompass more of who you can be.

Discipline – Making Loving Decisions

> 'Call them rules or call them limits...
> they are an expression of loving concern.'
> – Fred (Mister) Rogers

When your parents make a boundary for you, they are expressing their love for you, their desire to keep you safe. This is different to controlling you because they are afraid or not making any boundaries because they are lazy, disinterested or indifferent. Taking the responsibility and making the effort to make a boundary is an act of love. It has your happiness and well being at heart, as well as their own. They know you will both get on better with one another if a boundary is made. Because you have been respected enough to be disciplined and your parents have been self-disciplined enough to take control of the situation, this is how you learn self-respect and self-discipline.

As an adult, when you make a boundary, you are making a loving decision. This love indicates respect for yourself and the other person. Making boundaries is not an act of war. It is gentle, assertive, but not aggressive. War is aggressive and defensive, an attempt at power or control *over*. It follows you will have some kind of battle in your life if you do not make clear, firm, but gentle, boundaries.

Spoiled children have had permissive parenting, possibly alternating with controlling. They have had no boundaries made for them and so have been deprived of the experience of making their own. They are less likely to respect themselves and more likely to compensate this lack of self-respect and self-esteem with inflated ideas and fantasies about themselves, which are, in fact, empty, unfounded, and not true to their reality. They have an inadequate self-image and cannot define themselves. If you have been spoiled, as an adult, you may spend a lot of time trying to find out who you really are and where you really stand in the world. You probably have not learned to manage your impulses, contain your emotions or organise your resources adequately. You may well be gifted, but possibly underachieving, or achieving highly in order to please, but you may not be happy with your achievements because they are not what you really want to do most, which you are possibly denying. You may be using your achievements to compensate for the lack of love you felt as a spoiled child. Many spoiled children are given too much of what they do not need and not enough of what they do need – love, especially in the form of boundaries and discipline. Often they are given too much focused attention but not enough genuine love.

Discipline, which later becomes self-discipline, is satisfying. It feels good, not self-righteous or punishing. Boundaries, lovingly made, do not reject people, only behaviours. Sometimes making a boundary may hurt you more than the other person or people involved. This is known as, 'tough love,' or 'ruthless compassion.' When you act with compassion, that is, suffering with, you may have to make some sacrifices in order to do what you believe to be right, knowing that the outcome will be beneficial for all concerned. Do not confuse compassion with pity or sympathy, which sentiments do not always lead to clear boundaries. It is important to know that 'No,' is a complete sentence and that you have a right to say it, if you need to. When you make a boundary, you need to mean it. This is part of self-discipline. Making a boundary may cause pain in the short-term, but this will lead to pleasure in the long-term. Discipline often takes courage and courage, like love, comes from the heart.

Punishment or Consequences

> 'There are no rewards or punishments
> – only consequences.'
> – Dean William R. Inge

Discipline is not punishing. Punishment is abusive. Discipline is for your own good; punishment is not, whatever you may have been told. It causes unnecessary suffering, which is long-term pain. It is restricting, rather than limiting. It rejects people, not necessarily behaviours and comes from a hard and hateful place, often from a desire for vengeance or retribution. Punishment is shaming, which is abusive. It serves no purpose other than to subdue and humiliate, so it is a form of bullying. Sometimes one person may be punished because of a grudge against someone else. Whereas discipline is firm and gentle, punishment is harsh and unkind. When you think you are disciplining someone else, or yourself, examine your motives and check out whether what you are doing is discipline or punishment. If you are punishing yourself, did you learn to do this through guilt and shame?

Discipline is not bought through rewards. This is more likely to be obedience training through bribery. Obedience may be desirable when you want your own way in a hurry, but respect earned through making clear boundaries is more likely to engender long-term co-operation. It is more satisfying and less expensive too. If you have been indulged as a child, given rewards to placate you, which is not loving and does not promote your growth or well being, you may indulge yourself now as an adult. Think about the ill effects of self-indulgence in your life now. When you are indulging yourself, which is similar to comforting yourself, ask yourself what you really want and make some clear boundaries.

A more mature alternative to punishment is to consider the consequences of your actions. It is more helpful to learn the consequences of making boundaries, a reward in themselves, and the privileges that come from co-operation, than to be rewarded for obedience or placated for being a nuisance. The consequences of reward or placation will not necessarily give the same results in all circumstances; the results of making boundaries are more predictable. As an adult you have enough experience to be able to estimate the consequences of your actions. Then you are able to make choices. You know it is possible that if you commit a serious crime, your liberty will be taken away from you. This is not a punishment; it is a consequence of your actions. You have a choice.

If you grew up with parents who punished you when you displeased them or rewarded you for obedience, but did not make clear boundaries, firm but flexible rules, for you, you will not have a clear idea of consequences now. You are more likely to believe in hostility and defensiveness, or your ability to manipulate people instead of making an honest boundary. If you have not been taught how to contain your emotions, you will not know how to think before you act.

Rewriting Geraldine's Story

Geraldine realised she had little self-discipline, she was unable to make clear boundaries with her children or her husband and she felt victimised by all of them. She complained often but did not say what she wanted. I asked her to start making some boundaries by saying what she did want.

She said she wanted support with the children and the household duties. In fact, she was feeling like a single parent. She also wanted to be treated with respect by her children and her husband. We started to look at how she could reasonably ask for these things.

She asked her husband to share child rearing and decision making. Geraldine made a boundary by telling him she would no longer tolerate his abusive rages. Instead, they resorted to negotiation about their differences. Her husband confessed he had felt excluded from the family. He found that, by taking his share of the responsibility, he felt included. By letting go of sole control, Geraldine felt less burdened.

She realised her children wanted her attention in the afternoons, so she stopped work at four o'clock and spent an hour or so with them. Then they were allowed to play while she worked for another hour or so, but she made it clear that, if they were disruptive, they would be sent to their rooms alone. They accepted this arrangement without complaint.

After that, she got the children to help her prepare the evening meal. Her husband agreed to be home by half past seven and the family ate together. In this way he got to know his children better.

Geraldine reported that she was getting more respect from her husband and children, who all seemed happier. I explained that her children would feel safer because they knew where they stood with their parents, who now presented a united front. They also knew what would be tolerated and what the consequences of their actions would be; whereas, before, the threat of their father's anger was an unknown quantity.

Geraldine reported more love in her family. I also noticed that where she had been brittle and tense, she was now softening and becoming more feminine. She reported an improvement in her love life too. She realised this was because there was more trust between her husband and herself. She no longer feared his bad temper and she felt less resentment. She also found her children more affectionate and realised her sharp, attacking tongue had been a defence that pushed them away from her.

For You to Think About:

How clearly you make boundaries.
Your attitudes towards discipline and punishment.

> *'Teach us, O Lord, the disciplines of patience,*
> *for to wait is often harder than to work.'*
> *– Peter Marshall*

9

THE PATIENCE TO PERSEVERE

> 'The full fruit of a labour of love lives in the harvest,
> and that always comes in its right season.'
> – Narcotics Anonymous

Time

Time is a gift. When you are small you have no real conception of time or what you can do with it. When you are a baby, your needs are extremely urgent. Without food and attention you would not survive for very long. You need instant gratification. But, as your abilities increase, you can wait for longer periods of time, without anxiety, for your needs to be met. You know you will survive. As you grow up, your endurance increases, particularly your emotional and spiritual strength. You learn about working for things you want and the time that it may take for a task, process or creation to reach fruition. This comes with experience. As you gain a sense of who you are and build a life of your own, you learn to punctuate your time with work and play, activity and rest, with solitude and company, so that it does not feel endless or empty. You learn to organise your time, to wait for what you want and the time it takes to get it.

Patience, Suffering and Acceptance

> 'The best thing about the future
> is that it comes one day at a time.'
> – Abraham Lincoln

Time requires waiting. You have to wait for time to pass because things only materialise over time. As you learn the discipline of waiting, for satisfaction and fulfilment, rather than gratification, you learn patience. You learn to contain your impulses and emotions and use them creatively. You can harness your gifts and resources and apply them, over time.

You can only live one day at a time. You need not forget the past; you can learn from it. You can have hopes for the future, but you can only live in the present. In this way you can manifest your hopes and wishes. You will bring them into existence, over time.

Sometimes, you may find waiting painful and interpret this pain as suffering. Suffering means allowing. You need to allow time. Fear of disappointment can cause you pain. You may have been disappointed in the past and so expect the same to happen again; then waiting makes you anxious; you seek instant gratification. Because you are in pain, you become impatient, hoping that reaching your goal will end this pain. However, if you act impulsively, out of fear and urgency, without adequate consideration, you are more likely to make faulty decisions and create more pain. You will fulfil your expectations of disappointment. If you have not learned the value of patience or respect for time, you will repeat what you have learned in the past.

A positive aspect to suffering is that it brings experience. You learn to accept what is, to accept and tolerate limitations and to allow yourself to be who you are. You learn endurance and also to stretch yourself beyond your limitations, to expand your boundaries. However, you cannot go beyond your limitations until you have accepted them for what they are. If you can be patient, you learn to have faith and trust in your own abilities and in your own growth processes. Often, waiting brings an awareness of what your choices are and which decisions are appropriate. Unless you admit and allow your suffering, you will not learn the cause of it or find out how to change it. This requires time and patience.

> 'In the struggle between the stone and the water,
> in time, the water wins.'
> – Chinese Proverb

Limitations

Time is a boundary. It binds you in the present, but, because the present is ever changing, it becomes your future without you having to think about it. As I have said, change happens over time. Thus, if you live in the present, you are constantly building your future. If you are hankering after the past, or the future, you are not truly living in the present; it is more difficult to manifest your dreams and visions. You are wasting the time you do have. By fully living in the present, you are participating in the process of change. This makes you feel more powerful, because, through experience, you learn that you can influence change, rather than waiting for it to *happen* to you. As you grow you learn to regulate your life through time. You learn that you are limited to the present, but that the future will always come.

You learn to organise and divide time into manageable units, to pace yourself and choose how best to use your time; and about your own particular span of attention and when you need to take a break or change your activity. Thus you learn to use your time creatively; to use it as a boundary that contains you, rather than a limitation that restricts you.

When you learn the value of yourself and your abilities, you will also value the time you have and use it well, rather than complaining about the time you do not have. Conversely, valuing your time is a way of valuing yourself.

Coming to Terms with Disappointments

> *'If we will be quiet and ready enough,*
> *we shall find compensation in every disappointment.'*
> *– Henry David Thoreau*

Limitations have compensations. When your parents made rules for you, they were for your safety; but they were also so you could learn about your abilities and how best to use them. It is the same with disappointments. You grow through them. You will not always get what you think you want and, often, you may find that what you do get suits your needs better anyway. Disappointments come from having expectations, which are prone to frustration. I prefer to think in terms of hopes and wishes, which may or may not be fulfilled.

You learn from disappointments because they challenge you to look for other possibilities. When you encounter disappointments and limitations, you either learn to work with what is available to you, your own resources, or the resources around you, or you find ways to gain the resources you need. In this way you learn that there is more you can have than you originally thought possible.

So accepting disappointments and working within limitations helps you to grow, to feel more capable and more powerful, and to learn to value yourself and your resources.

Cosma Went to a Workshop

Cosma was a colleague of mine who signed up for a weekend workshop with a famous international speaker who had written a book about growing up. Cosma had a lot of experience working with adults who had not grown up properly. He knew several of his colleagues would be at the workshop and he was looking forward to sharing information and experiences in this format.

The weekend started on Friday evening, when the speaker spoke for two and a half hours about his work. Cosma was feeling somewhat bored but consoled himself with the thought that the workshop proper would start on Saturday morning and he would have more interaction with the other participants. On Saturday, the speaker spoke again for long stretches of time about himself and his work. There was no audience participation, as Cosma had anticipated. He was getting exasperated hearing the speaker talking constantly about himself and subjects Cosma already knew about.

At one point the speaker talked about learning to accept disappointments as being an essential part of growing up. This was a new idea to Cosma and a revelation because he realised he was having to accept the disappointment of the weekend not, in fact, taking a workshop format, but a lecture format. So he resolved to make the most of his time. He knew he had the option of going home early and missing the Sunday session, the last day, but he also knew he was enjoying being with his colleagues during the breaks. He decided to miss the Sunday morning lecture but to arrive in time for lunch with his colleagues. He went for a long walk instead and contemplated the nature of disappointment.

In hindsight, he told me, he was glad for the experience he did have because it taught him an unforgettable lesson about disappointments and how to deal with them. Cosma did not fall into powerlessness. He examined his choices and used them wisely.

Solitude

> *'I live in that solitude which is painful in youth, but delicious in the years of maturity.'*
> *– Albert Einstein*

As you grow, you learn to tolerate periods of time alone. As you get to know who you are, you also get to like yourself and learn to enjoy your own company. Being alone is not the same as feeling lonely. When you value yourself, you do not feel bad when you are alone. It is only when you feel separated from your self that you feel truly lonely, whether you are alone or not. One of the joys of growing up is the gift of solitude. Solitude is a way of using time creatively, just as time in relationship with others can be used creatively. When you are alone, you have no outside influences; you are not filling up your time with distractions. It is in the emptiness of solitude that your richness and resources can develop and mature.

So, limitation, patience, disappointment and solitude are all character strengthening. They allow you to become more of who you are, to develop yourself from your own resources, to fill yourself up from inside, rather than outside yourself and to discover what you are made of. They give you strength and endurance and teach you perseverance. They teach you about restraint, caution and also commitment, all of which depend on time. They teach you the benefits of going slowly and seeing processes through to completion and therefore fulfilment for you. Lastly, they teach you to like yourself.

For You to Think About:

How you use time.

> *'With love and patience,*
> *nothing is impossible.'*
> *– Daisaku Ikeda*

10

WORKING THROUGH THE PROBLEMS

> *'Decide what you want,*
> *decide what you are willing to exchange for it.*
> *Establish your priorities and go to work.'*
> *– H. L. Hunt*

Negotiation and Relationships

You do not live in isolation. Other people live in the same world as you. When you learn about independence, and find out who you are, you then learn about interdependence and your various relationships with other people. This is when you learn the difference between the concepts of *me* and *us* and make room for both in your life. It is not possible to live without coming into some kind of relationship with other people. Having a diversity of relationships is one of the joys of growing up that may not be available to you when you are small and your relationships are limited to members of your family.

In order to make boundaries, rules and commitments as well as joint agreements and to protect yourself in relationships with other people, you learn to negotiate. This is an area of adult life where you use your authority, integrity, power and autonomy, where you take responsibility for yourself and what you want in your life and where you work with limitations, both accepting them and overcoming them where possible. It is through negotiation that you may be able to go further than you originally think is possible when beset with a problem or disagreement. Negotiation is also a way of discovering choices.

One of the joys of growing up is learning how to negotiate through the open articulation of your thoughts, feelings and opinions, your hopes and wishes, your desires and needs, in dialogue with another person or persons, where you see your own and the other person's desires and needs as equally valid. In this way you may make compromises, but you do not compromise your self, your truth or your integrity, which is important if you want to avoid the accumulation of resentment. Negotiation is often a way of sharing and resolving problems. It needs a good sense of your self, plus a willingness to listen to and empathise with the other person or persons concerned. As a child or as an emerging adult you may not have had your needs and wishes validated or been given the opportunity to negotiate.

Negotiation can take time. It does not necessarily bring instant gratification, but it does bring satisfaction for all parties, a win/win result. It needs flexibility, the willingness to let go of what you think you need and to use what you can have creatively. It is a way of managing changes and uncertainty. Negotiation is dialogue and discussion between people that assumes friendliness, not enmity. Its purpose is reciprocity, which is both giving and taking, equality and mutual exchange with the aim of a common goal and mutual benefits. Negotiation needs co-operation. It follows that it promotes love, trust, intimacy and relatedness.

Negotiation is also a means of managing anger and resentment. Its aim is conflict resolution, not collusion. It results in contracts and agreements. All of this is possible between a parent and child, as well as between adults. Remember, if you have conflict within yourself, you can also negotiate with yourself.

Competition and Collusion

> *'Visible goodwill is the strongest negotiation strategy.*
> *Don't let somebody else determine your behavior.'*
> *– Dr. S. U. Sunrei*

Negotiation is a powerful tool; competitiveness is not. You negotiate *for* a common purpose, assuming goodwill and aiming to resolve problems, but you always compete *against* somebody; this implies opposition, rather than co-operation. You are at war and your aim is to win. Once you engage in battle you give your power away. In your attempt to undermine the other person, you defeat and undermine yourself. Fighting becomes self-perpetuating. You attack and blame, but you are less likely to state clearly what you want, or to articulate anger. You keep yourself impotent.

Many parents battle with their children in an attempt to control them. Unlike negotiation and co-operation, controlling is based on fear and engenders fear, not trust and love.

In competing, you use one-upmanship in an attempt to stay top dog. You can only do this by putting someone else down. Immature parents, and also teachers, do this to children. This means your feeling of power is dependent on the other person's weakness, powerlessness and submission. Such power is a, possibly shared, illusion. It is not true power because it is dependent on someone else. However pseudo-independent you may be, you are, in fact, *feeling* powerless and dependent and acting out those feelings. Children do not know this but many adolescents begin to sense it and fight back.

If you are competitive, you will try to use authoritarianism, bullying and manipulation, rather than true authority, openness and honesty to remain on top, to win. This takes more and more energy and may escalate into violence as you frustrate yourself more and more, as it did with Rachel and Keith. But, in a competitive situation, no one wins; and there is nothing to win anyway. Everybody loses because problems do not get resolved. All you achieve is enmity and possibly an illusion of control that is based on fear.

Competitiveness should not be confused with competition, which is a healthy response to challenge and is not at the expense of anyone else, even though other people are involved.

Competitiveness is a defence against feelings of powerlessness. You may use it to try to prevent change and to control uncertainty. It is based on the distorted belief that you *have* to compete to survive, to save face, which is really a façade, your false pride, that there is not enough power to go round and that power is something that can be 'won', rather than owned. If you have true power, it cannot be won or taken away from you. It is also based on the belief that you must control of be controlled. If there is co-operation, there is no need for controlling.

Collusion is a game of deception that two people play together; getting hooked in, often unknowingly, to a kind of mutual self-delusion, a shared distorted assumption. Competitiveness is a behaviour pattern you can so easily get hooked into, without knowing where or how the argument started. If you and the other person share the same distorted beliefs, you will collude with one another. This happens when you have not completed the transition through adolescence, when you believe that other people want to control you, when you have had competitive models and when you have not taken up your own power and authority. So check out your beliefs. It also happens when you react, rather than responding.

You can choose not to get hooked into competitiveness by detaching from this kind of behaviour when you become aware of it. This may be difficult in some relationships, because it means detaching from the other person. You do not have to fight. You can stand back, take up your authority and make a boundary, which is separating. You can also ask the other person to say clearly what they want. (You can use this tool in your relationship with yourself too). You will need to exchange rebelliousness and hostility for independence and integrity. If the relationship is a dependent one, you may not want to do this. If you are dependent on it for your sense of power, you may not want to separate and stand on your own two feet. This is also why many parents will not let go of their children – but children need to be allowed to grow up and adults need to be treated as adults, not children.

Do not forget that independence does not mean you cannot be in a relationship. But it takes two independent people to make a healthy, interdependent relationship.

Competitive relationships seem to me to be the most difficult to resolve. They fall into the 'can't live with them, can't live without them' category. Consequently, many people never mature beyond adolescence and live most of the time at loggerheads, preferring this situation to resolution that may bring change, and possibly separation, even though that change is more likely to be for the better. Through regressing into adult dependency by engaging in competitiveness, you surrender the independence and autonomy you are actually fighting for. In other words, your fear of dependency keeps you dependent – when you do have another choice; a choice that requires adequate models for maturity, including taking responsibility. At the same time, you may fear maturity – until you have models that are effective for you.

If you engage in competitive relationships, it is likely your parents did not negotiate with you when you were an adolescent, but tried to control you instead. Thus you have not learned to negotiate either. Through negotiation, you can reclaim your independence, autonomy and potency now. If you want to put people down, it is likely you have been put down yourself. By working with your self-image, you can change this behaviour.

Although negotiation and boundaries separate and individualise people, competitiveness actually keeps people apart. There can be no love or intimacy, no trust or relatedness – only collusion in competition and struggle, not together for a cause, but against one another, as in power struggle. Do not confuse collusion with co-operation. Competitiveness is neither supportive nor friendly; it creates rivalry and feelings of rejection and alienation, and low self-esteem. It assumes that the other person is the enemy, whoever they are, even a marriage partner.

> 'Real learning comes about when the competitive spirit has ceased.........
> This is true not only of competition with others,
> but competition with yourself.'
> – J Krishnamurti

It is possible to be your own worst enemy. And any relationship you have is unlikely to be any better than the one you have with yourself.

Neil and Jennifer

Neil and Jennifer were in their late thirties. They had known each other for six months when Neil moved into Jennifer's apartment, a year before they came to see me. They realised they would each have to make adjustments to living together. In many ways they got along very well domestically. However, there were certain conflicts they could not resolve. They would get hooked into arguments, which escalated.

Jennifer said she was beginning to see how Neil pulled her into power struggles when she asked him to do anything. She did not want to fight with him. She said she found these fights tedious and Neil said he found them traumatic. When she could not get Neil to co-operate, Jennifer would nag. She said her only other option was to detach, but then she felt they had no connection or relationship. When she nagged him, Neil found himself unable to articulate and Jennifer got angrier because she did not get explanations. She became indignant. Neither of them was being honest about their feelings.

Firstly, I instigated a no-blame rule. This meant that they both had to take responsibility for what they felt. Jennifer then admitted she found Neil emotionally unavailable and wanted more passion in their love life and less in their fighting. With permission to be honest and without feeling blamed, Neil was able to say that he felt overwhelmed by Jennifer's demands and therefore unable to relate at all.

It transpired that Jennifer's father had been preoccupied with his work when she was a child. She said she never felt able to reach him, but she had a strong relationship with her mother and four sisters; they mostly carried on family life without him and remained close as adults. She said she still longed for the father she never had and felt hurt and rejected by him.

Neil's mother was widowed when he was five. He had two sisters and felt his mother was dependent on him to be the man of the household, which he resented. When her nagging escalated into blaming and he felt the full weight of her despair and loneliness, he would escape and go for long walks alone. During the hardships of his childhood, he had learned to love his solitude.

It appeared to me that Neil was not able to compensate Jennifer for her lack of a father and Jennifer was not able to be the kind of mother Neil would have liked his mother to be. I explained that it was not appropriate for them to parent each other anyway.

I was able to help Neil to say he wanted to be able to have time alone, which he liked. Jennifer was then able to say she wanted more closeness. Through a process of negotiation they were able to find a way to co-operate with each other enough to have both relatedness and separateness, without taking exception to the other's needs. Jennifer came to understand that Neil was not abandoning her, as her father had done and Neil realised that Jennifer was not holding him responsible for her happiness, as his mother had done. Jennifer became more self-disciplined with Neil than she needed to be in her relationships with her mother and sisters and Neil recognised that engaging with Jennifer and sharing responsibilities would not mean loss of his power or independence as it had done with his mother. He, too, was able to make better boundaries in the relationship. Jennifer realised that Neil could be available emotionally if she respected his sensitivity and Neil accepted Jennifer's need for the closeness he had never had. In this way they both regained the love they had lost as children and felt more powerful and capable in their ability to generate this in their adult relationship. They were both satisfied with the results of their negotiations and both benefited from the resolution of their conflicts.

Neil and Jennifer got more than they originally believed they could have.

Co-operation

Co-operation is the outcome of making boundaries. When you have boundaries you also have no other choice than to co-operate. Negotiation involves co-operation, which is a shared effort, working together for mutual benefit, getting work done through collaboration. As with negotiation, you need to be flexible, open and willing to listen. If you are competitive you do not co-operate, share labour or benefits. Instead you collude, which is self-defeating. Co-operation and collusion are not the same. Collusion is used to maintain dependence and the illusion of power and control through the other person's weakness and need. Co-operation is essential to interdependence; it also requires, recognises and respects independence; but it does not require or support dependence.

> 'United we stand, divided we fall.'
> - Proverb

In fact, co-operation is far safer than competitiveness. It engenders trust and stability, even in times of change and uncertainty. It also leads to, supports and enhances creativity, whereas competitiveness can only be destructive, leaving no scope for self-expression because you hide your true self behind the role you play, inflated or deflated, oppressor or victim. Co-operation is a uniting of wills towards a common purpose, but competitiveness is a battle of wills.

If you did not learn and were not shown co-operation as a child and have not grown beyond childish tantrums or adolescent rebellion, as a grownup, you will not enjoy its benefits.

Conflict Resolution

> 'We cannot change anything until we accept it.
> Condemnation does not liberate, it oppresses.'
> – C. G. Jung

Conflict is a fact of life. It is healthy, constructive and brings greater meaning to your life and relationships. Conflict arises out of a need for change; it challenges you to grow. It is an attempt to find balance when change breaks down your old equilibrium and you are trying to find a new, more appropriate, state of balance that accommodates this change. Often the defensiveness that is so characteristic of competitive thinking is, in fact, an acting out of your inner, psychological conflict; usually conflict that you have not resolved in your growing up. You are in conflict with yourself. This is how the game of collusion gets played out, which can be seen in the stories of Rachel and Keith in Chapter Four, Desmond and Sandra in Chapter Five, and Neil and Jennifer in this chapter.

Essential elements of conflict are the need for change, uncertainty, needing to find focus and direction and the need to let go of behaviours, attitudes or assumptions, including distorted thinking, very often false pride, that have become redundant. It is also about making, often difficult, choices. Conflict is the working through of grief that comes with letting go and moving on. But this grief is sweet and releasing. If you deny the presence of conflict and avoid addressing it, you will not grow, even though you may have a reasonably peaceful life, but you will probably always feel something is missing from it. If you do admit and address conflict, it is possible that past and present, internal and external conflicts will be resolved at the same time. Current circumstances often trigger old conflicts. This kind of regression to childhood feelings happened for Desmond and Sandra.

> *'Elusion is a way of getting round conflict without direct confrontation, or its resolution.'*
> *– R D Laing*

If you are competitive, you are trying to resolve conflict by blaming rather than taking responsibility; by controlling, rather than taking control. You are trying to avoid the pain of an old, unresolved conflict, which includes feelings of powerlessness. In this way you cause even more conflict. You could say that adolescent rebellion is driven by the pain of having to let go of childhood and feelings of impotence in the face of adulthood; it is the fear of dependence, combined with the fear of being controlled and the ignorance of available choices. In eluding the real conflict you also prevent its resolution. You may confront people, but not problems, which need to be identified before they can be addressed. Blaming oppresses. You may have a sense that something is missing, perhaps a part of yourself, and you do not know how to find it, so you blame the other person. If only they would change, you will feel better. You are not being truthful with yourself, facing your own conflict and therefore the opportunity to liberate your self, to reclaim what you feel is missing. It is inside, not outside of you.

Try these steps to resolving conflict in relationship with someone else, or with yourself: stand back from that relationship or the conflict, without blaming yourself or the other person. Then ask:

- What am I feeling?
- When did I first feel this in my childhood?
- In what primary relationship?
- Who first judged and criticised me and taught me to do this to myself?
- Who first gave me competitive goals and false standards to live up to?
- Are they appropriate for me now?
- Do they matter anyway?
- How is self-doubt and false pride driving me in my relationship conflict?
- Can I change my competitive beliefs by letting go of a) this false pride and b) the need to live up to false standards that are not appropriate for me?
- How can I make amends to the person I am blaming?

Also ask yourself:
- Do I feel oppressed?
- Who do I believe is trying to control me?
- How?
- What choices do I have now that I did not have as a child or adolescent?
- Who tried to control me then?
- How great was the threat?
- How great is it now?

Remember, you have the gifts of articulation, communication, negotiation and explanation.

Once you have identified the conflict within yourself, you might like to set up an imaginary dialogue between your true self and your false self, the person who gave you the inappropriate values that have become your false and judgemental self or the person who tried to control you. You will soon realize how redundant values, beliefs and fears are causing you conflict and holding you back. Remember that controlling, judgements and jealousy are all based on fear, not trust. Who was afraid of you? Who is now? And why? Remember that co-operation is based on love. If you try to avoid inner conflict you waste time and energy fighting with yourself, or someone else. You need to let go of images of yourself that no longer fit. You will find this is a relief and immediately releases creative energy. Conflict resolution requires flexibility and an open mind.

Another way of avoiding conflict is to regress to dependency, either wanting comfort in a relationship or trying to indulge yourself. This does not lead to satisfaction and fulfilment and may lead to addictions. You will also make yourself feel even more powerless and frustrated and are unlikely to achieve anything creative. Self-indulgence and dependency are ways of dealing with current conflicts as if they were those old, developmental conflicts. Conflicts are merely growing pains. They can be painful, but you can grow through them. Staying in them creates far more pain, which is hard and enduring, instead of healing and releasing.

Another way of dealing with conflict is for one person to make unrealistic demands, to nag, and the other to withdraw. If you are making unrealistic demands of the other person, you are not facing your own pain. If you are withdrawing, you are avoiding emotions you do not know how to express potently, particularly explosive rage. This is how Rachel and Keith dealt with their conflict, inner and outer; so did Neil and Jennifer. The demand/withdraw strategy is another form of competitiveness, of attempting to maintain power and control; it is self-defeating. You need to accept that you do not have control over another person, only yourself. If you use the demand/withdraw approach you are holding onto your power, when you could be using it to resolve your conflict in the ways I have talked about.

Many couples regress to competitiveness when they have not learned how to manage their gender identity and mature sexuality. They nag or withdraw because they do not know how to or dare not ask for what they want. They may not know what they can have and may not expect to get it even if they do.

> *'It isn't that they can't see the solution.*
> *It is that they can't see the problem.'*
> *– G K Chesterton*

Resolution of conflict, including necessary grieving, is the completion of a task, which then enables you to move on. That is why it requires co-operation; including co-operation with your true self, instead of your false self. In other words, you need to listen to yourself and your instincts; not to the punishing, controlling, oppressive and judgemental, rejecting parental voices that have become your own. You do know what is true and what is right for you. You also know when you are negating that as they or others may have negated it – for whatever reason. You know what you feel. Competitive behaviour, putting other people down, is based on jealousy and disappointment, sour grapes, as well as fear of the other person's power. It is OK to admit your disappointments and to say what you want. You stand no chance of getting it if you will not even admit it.

Resolution of conflict may take you through periods of uncertainty before the task is completed. This calls for patience and perseverance, a certain amount of endurance and respect for timing and limitations; and, most of all, listening. Resolving conflict usually enables you to overcome limitations and achieve results you never before believed were possible. This is the miracle of negotiation and co-operation, both of which entail going into unknown territory and trusting. That also means trusting yourself and your ability to make boundaries, use your authority, wait, negotiate and co-operate where appropriate; as well as asking for what you want.

Change

The importance of changes that come about through negotiation and co-operation is that they lead to greater complexity; in other words, more choices. Negotiation and co-operation allow for positive feedback, which helps you to grow. The negative feedback of competitiveness does not help you to grow, or change positively, which happens only when you stop trying to control the outcome of change. This means allowing someone else's position, even if it is your true self, into the equation; that is, allowing reciprocity. This also highlights the importance of interdependent relationships in grown up life; and, most importantly, your relationship with yourself. The process of negotiation itself helps you to see your outworn behaviour and to let it go, thus making changes within yourself. It opens your mind to multiple possibilities, including your own hopes and wishes.

Information, Communication and Articulation

The gift of negotiating helps you to practice communication and articulation, which are gifts of being grown up. They make you feel more powerful and capable, as do the outcomes of negotiation and co-operation. Communication is organised and punctuated through articulation, which is your tool for making boundaries and how you choose to convey information. It is important that this articulation is open and honest.

When you are competitive you do not give information; you give commands, criticisms and possibly conflicting information. Your aim is to control through manipulation. You do not tell the truth, even to yourself, because you have learned to compete with yourself in an attempt to live up to the judgements you make about yourself; and possibly to stay one-up in your old struggle against the control of parents and others. You do not resolve conflict because you believe that, if there is resolution, one person wins and the other loses; and you are also powerless to win. You are afraid of losing power and control, so you withhold information, even from yourself. Withholding information does not give you power, it only keeps you one-up, a position that is difficult to maintain. Healthy communication that leads to successful negotiation and benefits all parties needs explanation, clarification and elucidation, not blame. It is not possible to negotiate without information. If your parents used controlling instead of negotiation and articulation of information, you will have learned to be competitive. This keeps you stuck in adolescence.

Articulation is a more potent means of managing emotions than withholding and sulking or acting out and exploding. It is also a better way to get help, support and co-operation, and to enable change, so that you do not get stuck in immature emotions and can move into maturity. Accepting what is, which is necessary for conflict resolution, also needs listening, elucidation and explanation, not blaming. Were you listened to as a child or adolescent? More importantly, do you listen to yourself now?

For You to Think About:

How you negotiate and how you co-operate.
The competitive standards you may live by.

> *The greatest conflicts are not between two people*
> *but between one person and himself.'*
> *– Garth Brooks*

11

WHAT ARE NEGATIVE EMOTIONS?

> *'There can be no transforming of darkness into light
> and of apathy into movement
> without emotion.'*
> *– Carl Gustav Jung*

Emotions are Physical Feelings

Emotions are one of the greatest causes or triggers of conflict, in your relationships, but particularly within yourself. You can choose to battle with your emotions, or you can choose to acknowledge, allow and respect them; and to learn how to manage them.

Emotions are messages your brain sends to various parts of your body, which is where you *feel* them, roughly speaking, in your head, your heart or your belly, depending on what they are. Emotions are physical *feelings*. Even though the word 'emotion' is usually used to describe feelings more passionately expressed and the word 'feeling' is used to describe feelings that are softer and more sensitive, they are all emotions that you *feel*. They arise spontaneously, without your conscious effort, as a response to a stimulus. It is in the first five years of your life that you learn your responses to given stimuli. These learned responses are stored in your memory.

Generally speaking, emotions are a healthy, passionate expression of your life force. You cannot prevent yourself from feeling them, although you may deny, or be unable to interpret, what you feel; or you may divert healthy passion into destructive action if you are not able to direct it constructively. All emotion can be used constructively, to act or to heal. Healthy emotions are a response to what is going on around you; they arise out of your basic human needs for safety, survival and socialisation, which are physical, emotional, intellectual and spiritual, as I explained in Chapter Three. If these needs have not been met in childhood, your responses to certain stimuli may be out of proportion.

Emotions move you. You feel them as an impulse to act. You have emotions so you can register and interpret what is going on around you. They inform you about your reality, but the responses you learned to certain stimuli in your early years, especially if those stimuli were more than you could cope with or less than you needed, can distort your interpretation of this reality. If your emotions are intense and highly charged, driving you, and out of proportion to what is happening in the present, it is possible that events in the present are triggering memories of, often traumatic, events in the past that you did not learn to manage, or were not able to respond to, appropriately. Because you did not have the ability to interpret these events logically at the time, you could only respond emotionally. If you attempt to identify what you are feeling, then you can put it into perspective now, heal the past by feeling and understanding it, and learn to better manage your emotions in the present.

> *'For humans, there is a small space between stimulus and response, and in this space lies the power to make choices that will determine the course of our lives.'*
> *– Unknown*

Until you have learned to recognise, respect and manage your emotions, some of them may be too instant for thought to intervene before you act. Others may come slowly and be more tender. They may touch you, rather than move you, giving you time to choose what to do about them, if you recognise what they are.

One of the joys of growing up is learning to contain your emotions, so that you consider what you are feeling before you act. You also have the gifts of communication, articulation, logic and reason, so you need not 'act out' physically or non-verbally, even though this is your initial impulse. You can consider and then verbalise what you are feeling, which you could not do as a baby. Babies express their emotions purely non-verbally, through their bodies; they do not think about them first. As an adult you have other choices. Nevertheless, expressing emotion now does not mean you are a baby. You are more likely to be a baby if you do not have the courage to do so. Hopefully, as you were growing up, you were taught to say how you felt or what you wanted, rather than being allowed to act out. This is the best way to deal with tantrums, just as negotiation is the best way to deal with adolescent rebellion, providing childhood tantrums have been mastered first. Hopefully, you were also taught to consider the consequences of your actions. If you do not communicate your feelings in relationships, the other person is left to guess, which, even if they are good at reading body language, does not lead to clarity, which is essential in healthy relating.

The other joy of growing up is the ability to respect what you feel and accept it as your authority about you. Hopefully, your feelings were respected as you were growing up. Even a baby knows how it feels, even if it cannot rationalise or articulate it; and most babies manage to convey their feelings by the tone of their crying. That is why they can be expressed non-verbally, even though this may not be the most appropriate way to do it when you are grown up, except in an emergency. Maternal instinct may have enabled your carers to interpret what you wanted when you could not speak, and to use their own logic to decide what to do about it, but it is not fair to expect other people to guess what you want or how to supply it when you are an adult, even in a dependent relationship. Adult desires tend to be more complex than those of babies anyway.

Acting Out and Acting In, Containing or Controlling

If you were not taught how to manage your emotions, you may have been allowed to act out, to 'explode', which is traumatic and later leads to violence. This does not direct emotion into constructive action. If you were not allowed to express emotion or your emotions were negated or denied, you may have learned to withhold your feelings and possibly sulk. You will deny your feelings now and probably not be aware of them, or know what they are. This also does not lead to resolution or creative expression and may result in physical or mental illness. Neither method is healthy. Withholding and denial are ways of acting in, rather than acting out, of 'imploding', and therefore lead to violence against yourself. Neither acting out, acting in or denial helps you to value yourself, gain self-respect or maintain self-esteem. All are ways of dealing with frustrated needs that only serve to frustrate you further. If you are acting out, you are not containing your emotions and if you are acting in, you are controlling them. If you have had good boundaries made for you and have learned self-discipline, you know how to contain what you feel and decide how to act on it appropriately. You know how to respond, rather than react. You can make these boundaries for yourself now. It is never too late for self-parenting, but it needs to be appropriate to your present age.

It's OK to feel deeply moved
by the intensity of your own feelings.

Emotions are human, so their recognition, allowing and expression bring people closer together. When you act out, you push people away from you. When you act in, you have a barrier around you. Both are defensive. Emotions are a gift and, used constructively, rather than destructively, bring richness and fulfilment to your life. Although the emotions that are known as positive, LOVE and JOY, initially make you feel better than those that are known as negative, FEAR and PAIN, all emotions are ultimately positive because, if you use them constructively, they move you and therefore lead to growth and change. The only truly negative emotions are those that are used destructively or are held in and allowed to stagnate and fester.

Containing your emotions, not acting immediately you have the impulse, but also not denying and controlling them, allows you time to process what you are feeling, interpret it and then decide what you want to do with it. You have a choice. You can use logic to understand your emotions, but beware of using logic to deny emotion. Both logic and emotion are equally important. In the same way, rationalising will help you to manage and understand your emotions, but be careful not to rationalise them away, which then becomes irrational because you are denying what you are feeling, together with the opportunity to change something that is making you uncomfortable or unhappy; or enjoy something that *is* making you happy.

Dealing With Rage and Anger

> 'Love is what we are born with.
> Fear is what we learn.'
> – Marianne Williamson

Love and fear are the basic, primary emotions in humans. All others are variations. Rage is a *reaction against* and anger is a *response to* pain and fear. You are more likely to feel rage when your basic survival or your will are attacked and more likely to feel anger when your rights or your identity are attacked; but you may feel rage in all these situations, depending on how helpless you feel, how much you have grown up and how much you are denying the pain you feel. It is important to know the difference between rage and anger, even though rage is often called anger. Rage acted in or acted out is destructive; acted out it is noisy and explosive, whereas anger can be expressed quietly, gently and with respect. It is not punishing, blaming or shaming. Rage is more likely to drive you. Anger gives you more time to think.

Acting out rage is abusive; it is hard and unloving; it is hot, but leaves you feeling cold and lonely. Abusiveness is a no-win strategy, and, like competitiveness, it escalates. At the most it gives a shaky victory, which is dependent on superior physical strength or weaponry, sometimes on intellectual strength. It may lead to an uneasy truce, based on fear, but there is no real resolution of conflict.

> 'I was angry with my friend I told my wrath, my wrath did end.
> I was angry with my foe: I told it not, my wrath did grow.'
> – William Blake

Expressing anger is a way of taking responsibility for what you feel, but handing back responsibility for what has been done to you, putting responsibility for actions and behaviours, including blaming and shaming, where it belongs. This can be gentle and loving.

Anger is cool, but leaves warm feelings. It can transform enemies into friends.

Rage

Rage belongs in childhood. It is pre-verbal. It is the primal response to pain and the fight response to fear. As such it is a survival mechanism for babies when fear and pain threaten to overwhelm them. Then it is better to fight than to lose your sanity or worse, die. Toddlers use the same behaviour until they have learned to articulate. When you do not articulate fear and pain, but turn it inwards as rage, you become depressed because you have lost your fight. It is there, but you are fighting yourself because you are not articulating your rage by expressing it as anger. Anger is always behind depression. Basically, you are not saying what you want. You feel impotent.

In its extreme, rage is an impulse to kill, hence the term 'murderous rage'. Hatred and vengeance are products of rage and also of fear. Rage is always *against* something or someone. It is self-perpetuating and can be addictive. Rage is an avoidance and denial of pain and fear; it can be used to mood alter, to fill up emptiness and to avoid taking responsibility or decisive action. Raging is a way of blaming someone else, rather than admitting what you are feeling; you deflects your pain and fear outside of yourself or turn it inwards as denial of your feelings. It can be a red herring and a smoke screen. It prevents you from resolving problems and from growing up. Because anger makes boundaries that distinguish your individuality, you may use rage as a defence against separating and relinquishing dependency, which then keeps you in the vicious cycle of being dependent, raging against dependency, feeling helpless and alienated. If you cannot act out your rage, you take it out on yourself. You rage internally; either way you keep yourself trapped in the helplessness and dependency you are raging against.

Anger separates but, unlike rage, it does not alienate.

You may be raging against the pain and the fear of having your will thwarted, your inability to act, feelings of impotence, powerlessness and dependency, of feeling controlled and trapped, and against disappointment. Your rage may be about infringement of your rights, about wrongs and injustices, hurts, abuse in its many forms. Today it is less likely to be about your survival.

Rage is usually belly centred and hot. It is a primal emotion. It has not been refined through your heart. It is a move away from your heart when your heart is hurt. For many people, rage is easier to bear than emotional pain. Rage can feel murderous, because you want to wipe out what you feel is wiping you out, what is threatening your sense of self. Rage makes you feel 'bad' and therefore unreal and 'crazy'. You do not feel authentic or mature. This is not fulfilling. You want to hurt what or who is hurting you, often just to stop it. You want to lash out, usually without thinking. This only gives temporary relief.

Rage is usually based on distorted thinking, a faulty belief in your helplessness. Except in extreme circumstances, you do have tools to overcome many of the things you may rage against. You have the gifts of communication, negotiation, articulation and co-operation and the ability to gather facts and to think for yourself. You also have the ability to move away from what is hurting you or making you feel unreal and 'crazy', not to engage with it, if you choose. You may not be as helpless as you think you are. But you may be feeling as helpless as you once were. It is important to check out the difference between then and now and then to take up your authority and your power.

When Rachel Left Keith

> 'Usually when people are sad, they don't do anything.
> They just cry over their condition.
> But when they get angry, they bring about a change.'
> – Malcolm X

Although it is important to feel pain and to grieve, if that is what you are feeling, it is also possible to collapse into helplessness and self-pity, indulging yourself in tears, rather than admitting anger and making a boundary. Anger is a great motivator. It is a positive force, not to be confused with revenge.

If you look at the story of Rachel and Keith in Chapter Four, you will see how Keith raged against the pain of rejection by becoming violent with Rachel and then collapsed into helplessness.

It was only when he stopped idealising the memory of his early childhood and his difficult adolescence and accepted that he had felt constantly rejected by his parents that Keith was able, through feeling the pain, to transform his rage into anger and make some clear statements about what he wanted for his life. I encouraged him to write letters to his parents, which he did not send, telling them how angry he felt about their inadequate parenting and the pain he had felt all his life because he had been unable to get the love he wanted, the love they had deprived him of. He was not able to love himself adequately because of the rage he carried; it did not serve his self-esteem. He felt ashamed and indignant, without really knowing why.

Keith was also able to see how his parents used raging, violence and alcohol to manage their feelings of fear and pain. He had copied their behaviour. Although we agreed that feeling rage and pain were better than the numbness he had become accustomed to, he was, in fact, falling into feelings of helplessness and indulging himself in weeping. He was an educated and articulate man, yet he could not verbalise his own needs and feelings because he had never learned, or even dared, to ask for what he needed as a child. He had grown up assuming it would not be forthcoming. To compensate, he had pretended not to need and had chosen a wife who appeared to need him. In therapy, Keith learned to convert fear and pain into anger, to pull himself up out of his depression by articulating how he felt, rather than acting it out, or in. He did not get his wife back because she had moved on, but he became much happier living with himself and lost the feelings of shame he was trying to mask with his pseudo-independent façade.

Anger

The ability to express anger is a gift of being grown up. It arises out of *feeling* your pain and fear and then using your authority and power. You learn to stand up for yourself and your rights, even in the face of threat, when that is appropriate, and to attempt to change what is harming or threatening you. You can express anger by making boundaries, by saying who you are and where you stand. This requires verbal communication and articulation, a sense of identity, knowing yourself (who you are) and allowing and understanding your feelings (where you stand); literally, where you are in your body. It also involves taking responsibility for what you feel, and being able to describe it. If in doubt, keep it simple; hurt, frightened and angry are easily understandable words and common human experiences. You can add more words to your vocabulary later on, like furious (for rage), rejected, abandoned, shamed, violated, humiliated, abused or plain uncomfortable when something does not feel right to you. Oh, and do not forget frustrated.

Anger is cooler and less urgent than rage. It is heart-centred and therefore requires courage, to feel pain and fear and to speak up. It is the only way to deal with the uncomfortable feelings of rage, which usually make you feel BAD – indignant. Anger is dignified. If you continue to rage, you will believe you are bad, which you are not. However, in the absence of tools in childhood for converting hot and destructive rage into cool, clear and constructive anger, and therefore having the chance to make changes, many people grow up believing they are essentially flawed. It follows that it is not good for you to rage. It is shaming and humiliating because it leaves you feeling impotent. It is undignified. Only anger can be focused and directed into creative, potent expression. Rage has a habit of going nowhere. I do not believe in leaving children to rage without helping them by giving them tools and helping them to articulate their needs and desires. This is abusive and traumatic, as well as neglectful and humiliating.

Nor do I believe in beating cushions. I have tried it. Nevertheless, there are many excellent physical therapies that do not repeat original trauma or humiliation and do help to gently access deeply buried emotions; but I do not believe in forcing material out of denial. I believe you will only allow into consciousness as much as you are emotionally able to deal with at any time. So do not force yourself. Be gentle. This is not a plumbing model. You do not have to regurgitate all your 'stuff' at once in order to heal or to grow. Growing and healing are processes that function alongside one another and they happen over time; in fact, they have a timing of their own. This timing is also co-ordinated with your growing consciousness, awareness and understanding. Integrating what you are feeling will heal your pain faster than forcing yourself, which may create pain; it is pain that creates the urgency to find solutions. Be patient.

All the same, it is important to feel rage, or any other emotion, if that is what you are experiencing. Feeling and acting out are not the same. After all, if you do not know what you are feeling, how will you be able to deal with it? But once you have felt rage, it is important to ask yourself why you are feeling it. Have you been hurt, or are you feeling hostile, defensive or frustrated, and, if so, what are you afraid of and what is frustrating you? The next question is, 'What can I do about this?' You are probably not as helpless as you believe yourself to be.

Other Forms of Anger

Resentment accumulates when you do not express hurt as anger; then it repeats. It comes back later, like onions, in a form of delayed reaction, often ending in explosive rage when the pressure builds up. Then you probably express it inappropriately and out of its original context. Holding onto hurt makes you feel passive, a victim; you may end up oppressing someone else with it, sometimes covertly. Resentful people, especially those caught in dependency, often make everyone around them feel angry while denying that they are angry and smiling sweetly. It is a good idea to examine your belief in your right to feel angry. Do not forget, whatever you feel is real for you and you have a right to feel it. Logically, it cannot be any other way. Resentment that accumulates stagnates and makes you ill. If you are feeling resentful, it is time to change something in your life by making a boundary.

Other feelings that are often called anger are irritation and frustration, which are mild forms of raging, sometimes due to impatience, sometimes due to feelings of helplessness. You may feel indignation when your dignity has been offended. Threatening, bullying, shouting, abusiveness and violence are behaviours that are often referred to as anger but are, in fact, rage.

Paranoia, which is felt as extreme fear, is, in fact, anger that is denied and projected onto other people, who are then experienced as threatening. When your anger has become so frozen that you feel it only in your head, mostly in your eyes and the back of your head, then you have moved into the realms of fantasy. If you feel paranoid, in the first instance, ask yourself what your fantasy is, if there is anything genuine to fear, and then ask yourself what you are angry about. I will talk about this some more in the next chapter.

Differences between Rage and Anger

These are the major differences between rage and anger:

ANGER	RAGE
Is potent	Is impotent
For protection	For defence
Feels and heals pain	Denies and causes pain
Ends suffering	Prolongs suffering
Responsible	Irresponsible
Mature	Immature
Separates	Alienates
Empowering	Disempowering
Brings resolution	Brings no resolution
Feels good	Feels bad (shame)
Is clear and clean	Is messy
Is open-ended	Goes round in circles
Is standing up for rights/boundaries	Is a victim stance
Is constructive	Is destructive
Uses your own authority	May use external authority
Dignified	Humiliating

For You to Think About:

How you deal with rage and anger.
How you contain, express and articulate your emotions.

> *'Your task is not to seek for love,*
> *but merely to seek and find*
> *all of the barriers within yourself that you have built against it.'*
> *– A Course in Miracles*

12

A RECURRING STATE OF BEING

> *'Whatever you fear most has no power –*
> *it is your fear that has the power.'*
> *– Oprah Winfrey*

Fear and Anxiety

Fear is the opposite of love. Fear restricts, reduces and obliterates love. That is why it generates hate. You feel fear or anxiety when you anticipate impending pain or danger, real or perceived. Anxiety is about uncertainty and the future, but is often influenced by experiences in the past. Like worry, it can make you sick. Anger is a response to hurt and fear, to hate, to being *deprived* of love, as is anxiety. The words 'anger' and 'anxiety' both have their roots in pain, soreness, torment, sadness, distress, tightening, narrowing and choking. Both anger, or rather, rage, and fear reduce your capabilities, shock and paralyse you and block the 'positive' emotions – love and happiness.

Terror is the paralysis of fear, which can lead to paranoia, a mixture of rage and fear. Paranoia is frozen rage because the alternative would be too dangerous, violence or worse, retaliation and punishment. When rage goes cold in this way, you feel as if you are leaving your body. This is the basis of panic. If you have grown up with frozen rage, because you have not been able to act when you felt threatened, you will tend to be controlling, manipulating, calculating, watchful and possibly paranoid. You will rely on thinking more than feeling. To release frozen rage, it is important to *feel* your fears. If they are from the past, you have already survived what frightened you then, so there is far more likelihood of you coping with it now. You are more emotionally equipped and have the experience to be able to put it into perspective.

Fear and Pain

> *'No suffering is so enduring*
> *as that which you refuse to acknowledge.'*
> *– Nathaniel Branden*

Because fear restricts, it causes you pain; so does your resistance to change. This causes misery and suffering. It may be your false pride that feels threatened. However, pain is your friend. It tells you when something is wrong and needs changing. It alerts you to danger and, like anger, it also tells you that you are alive. Pain can be inspiring.

I do not suggest you seek out pain. Human beings do suffer. You can reduce your suffering in many ways, not the least by admitting it, but also, remember, you learn through suffering.

> *'The turning point in the process of growing up is when*
> *you discover the core of strength within you survives all hurt.'*
> *– Max Lerner*

Facing up to pain and fear opens up your life. It strengthens you. If you shrink away, you contract into anger and anxiety, if you do not admit you are hurting, you will not be able to deal with what is threatening you. If you deny pain, you numb yourself. In this way, you die a bit, you lose vitality and you prevent yourself from healing and becoming more whole. Your life and your spirit are alive within that pain. So, if you believe your life is worth fighting for, when you feel pain, you need to face it, make boundaries, hand back what is not your responsibility, express your anger, (not the same as acting it out), and take positive steps to make changes. This is why, the more pain you can release from your past, with respect for process and timing, the more you can move on in the present, the more you can grow up and realise your potential, and the more you can prevent pain in the future; the more love, joy and happiness you are likely to find. Your false pride is a denial of pain; it holds pain from the past, especially rejection. It holds you aloof from feeling this pain. It also keeps you feeling rejected, and in pain. That is why it is important to identify pain when you find it motivating your present. This will strengthen your belief in yourself.

Remember:
The pain you might feel by remembering cannot be any worse
than the pain you feel by knowing and denying.

Remember, also, that you have already survived this pain when your physical and emotional resources were far less than they are today, even if you did have to freeze that pain at the time. You will feel far more pain by attempting to avoid it, than you will by facing it, and fear, full on. It is also likely you will cause pain to people around you if you deny your own. You tend to hurt people when you are hurting, even if you do not intend to. You will repeat the experiences that brought that pain to you. This has been illustrated by many of the stories I have recounted in this book.

Courage Is Good For Your Heart

'Courage is not the absence of fear,
but rather the judgement
that something else is more important than fear'
– Ambrose Redmoon

Courage is a gift of maturity. It is the willingness to take considered risks, not to be confused with bravado, which is a reaction *against* fear that is acting out without consideration. Many people consider it a weakness to admit to feeling emotional pain; some even to physical pain. This is competitive thinking (see Chapter Ten). In fact, it takes courage to allow yourself to feel emotional pain, and fear. Courage strengthens your heart. If you open your heart to allow pain, you will ultimately feel love, which, unlike fear, is expansive. Love is probably the most powerful, and healing, emotion there is. You could say it is more important than fear. Through courage, fear is transformed back into love, healing takes place and you grow nearer to your authentic self. What could be more important to you than your self? Courage is something you gain as you develop your physical, emotional, intellectual and spiritual resources, as you gain strength through experience, perseverance and endurance, by accepting suffering but not wallowing in misery; through acting when you can. Your other option is to prolong pain by contracting into anxiety and rage, acting out *against* pain and fear, which is painful, and restricting your choices, potential and ability to love. It is important to identify the source of your pain so that you know what you are dealing with. It is not necessary to blame.

When you open your heart to pain and fear, you also open it to love and joy. The process of growing up takes you from being belly-centred, where you feel rage and indignity and where you are mainly concerned with yourself and your needs, to your heart, where you allow yourself to feel pain and fear and from where you relate with others, because children are more concerned with wilfulness, with establishing their power and getting their own way, and adults are more concerned with will. I will talk about this will in the next chapter. Children do feel through their hearts. They do feel fear and pain. But they are not centred there. When you are heart-centred, you can then express anger as I have described in Chapter Eleven, through articulation, negotiation and co-operation. Thus you develop compassion for yourself and others. You create a world with love in it where you can express yourself safely and creatively to the best of your abilities; where you can develop your resources and share them with others. This process, like all maturing processes, can start in childhood.

Love is not based on greed, or need, but on an openness to give and receive. Rage, based on fear, is self-centred. Love means allowing all emotions without judging, containing them and choosing how to express them or transform them, focussing and channelling them creatively, rather than destructively and wastefully. If you expect love, you will find it, even though you may have to accept loss and disappointment along the way. Learning how to let go, when you need to, strengthens you.

You may not have got all the love you expected as a child but you can create it yourself now and it will be effective. It will influence people around you, even if your love did not seem to be effective when you were a child, because now you have the tools of adulthood you did not have then.

When you become heart-centred, you do not ignore your physical impulses, nor do you let your heart rule your head. You use your intelligence to consider your physical urges and temper them with love through your heart before deciding how to act on them. This is how you become a whole person. The marriage of your head, heart and belly become the sum total of your being, bound together, if you like, by your spirituality. You do need to use all your functions in balance.

Love and Longing

> 'Love is, above all, the gift of oneself.'
> – Jean Anouilh

Love never hurts. Only pain hurts. Loss hurts and needs to be grieved. Longing is often confused with love. It is the *pain* of 'falling' in love, which is really falling in longing, rather than the *joy* of 'being' in love, which grows over time, as you get to know the other person; you may believe you love them when you hardly know them. You cannot love what you do not know. It follows that getting to know yourself means growing to love yourself; delighting in your own company. This means that you can more easily choose friends and partners in whose company you also delight.

What you see when you fall in longing is your own reflection, something you believe you have lost, the gift of yourself. You think that someone else will compensate for what you believe you are lacking, rather than complementing who you already are. These feelings are more likely to be about the past than the present. If you feel longing, it is important to identify what you are longing for and to allow the grief at having originally lost it, whether it is your mother's love, your father's love or your own sense of self, which was dependent on their love. Then you will find you can reclaim what you believe you have lost. This may be a part of yourself, possibly once represented by or projected onto a parent, or the dream of a life you have grown to believe is impossible. This dream may need reshaping, but it is important to realise you believed you had lost it. You cannot live your life or fulfil your potential through another person. You need to do it for yourself, just as you need to learn to love yourself if you want to attract and create genuine, mature love in your relationships.

> *Remember:*
> *Love is not dependent on someone else.*

Toby Fell In Longing

Toby was an angry young man, even though he was in his mid thirties. He looked scruffy and seemed to be hiding, hunched inside his baggy, teenager's clothes and hooded anorak. He came from a wealthy family, was intelligent and had a good education but he had difficulty holding down a job and was unemployed when he came to see me. He had had many brief encounters with women and used sex addictively. He seemed to be enraged and very unhappy.

When he was a child, his parents had employed a series of nannies for Toby and his brothers, but had not paid much attention to their children themselves. They were usually busy socialising and sometimes having affairs. We worked through a lot of anger about emotional deprivation in his childhood and he wrote many letters to his parents, which he did not send. He even had some success in mending his relationships with them through letters and visits.

Eventually Toby embarked on some training and found a job he liked in the theatre. He also began a new relationship with Linda, which was promising to be stable, in which he was able to allow intimacy and make some good boundaries. However, after six months he ended the relationship because Linda began to see other men, which he was not willing to tolerate.

He did not regret this relationship, as it was such an improvement on his previous encounters, but he was still longing for Linda and obsessing about her. One day he brought two photographs to our session, explaining that he had had a revelation. One photograph was of Linda and the other, he explained, was a rare family photograph with his parents, his brothers and himself at fifteen. He showed me the similarity in looks between Linda and his mother. Both looked like attractive teenagers. Toby explained that, although his mother had been emotionally unavailable in his childhood, he realised that, when he became an adolescent, he had fallen in love with her from a distance. We deduced that his heart had been broken at that time because he knew there could never be intimacy between them, sexual or otherwise. Previously studious, from then on he had become a difficult teenager.

Although Toby had been raging about his childhood, it was as an adolescent he felt most rejected and broken-hearted. He had been raging against that pain ever since. His rage was a smoke screen. It was only when he worked through his childhood rage that he was able to have an intimate relationship. It was not by accident he chose a woman who then reminded him of his mother. He needed to heal that original wound, even though he had not been aware of this. I noticed after that realisation, which was so meaningful, although very painful for Toby, he gained confidence and took more pride in his appearance. He seemed to grow up and mature into a man quite suddenly. When I last saw him he told me he was not looking for a relationship, which had been his obsession since adolescence. Although he still wanted to marry and have children, he said he no longer needed someone else to love him because he felt able at last to love himself. He no longer felt the shame he had been carrying around and hiding since he was fifteen.

If Toby had experienced a loving relationship with his mother, he might have been able to treat his attraction to her, which was not love but longing, differently. She might have been able to help him if she had not, emotionally, been a teenager herself, but had been able to recognize and affirm Toby's emerging masculinity and sexuality. In a way, his longing for her at fifteen was really a longing for himself, a self that had never been recognised by his parents. He had been hiding that self ever since. His work in the theatre and his relationship with Linda gave him an opportunity to begin to express his true self, instead of hiding it behind his false pride, which took the form of adolescent rebellion, right into his mid thirties and was a defence against a broken heart. More than the loss of his mother's love, or the disappointment of his relationship with her, Toby was grieving for his own lost self, which he had projected on to her and which she neglected to affirm.

Love and Joy

> 'Fear is a dark room where negatives are developed.'
> – Patricia O'Gorman and Philip Oliver-Diaz

Fear robs you of joy, which is your natural state. Distorted beliefs and assumptions create fear and obscure love and joy. When you feel full of life, full of love and joy, you also feel excited. It is quite common, at the same time to feel fear. Excitement and anxiety often come together. This is because you have not learned to contain your joy and channel your excitement into creative activity. As a child, your natural exuberance and spontaneity may have been inconvenient in your family. You may have been punished for being too lively, or you may have grown up with depression in your family and been left fearing that love or joy will be snatched away from you or annihilated by parental disapproval and negativity. If your parents were afraid of life, they would have been afraid to let you be alive and tried to dampen down your vitality. Now you dampen down your positive feelings in anticipation of rejection. It is important for you to know that your joy is natural and healthy and that you are also entitled to it, even if other people are unhappy; it is your birthright. No one can take your love away from you. It is yours to keep and share appropriately. It is not necessary for you to make your parents' disappointments your own, even though they may have tried to do that to you inadvertently.

Joy is an impulse, and, like all emotions, usually needs consideration before action. If your spontaneous love was rejected as a child, you may be fearful of loving spontaneously as an adult. You may not believe in it and may be afraid to be joyful. If you have not learned to discriminate, you may love inappropriately, or you may incriminate because you do not trust adequately.

'Joy is but the sign that creative emotion is fulfilling its purpose.'
– Charles Du Bos

Healthy Aggression and Assertion

Aggression is healthy. It is your joy, your life force, your vitality, the energetic activity of your mind and body, which needs focussing and channelling into creative self-expression and the use and perfecting of skills. It does need containing so that it can be used properly and not dissipated. Frustrated aggression leads to raging, violence and destruction; so does boredom. This is why human beings need to work. Work is as creative for adults as play is for children, and not dissimilar. It is through the repetitive activity of play that children learn skills. Practising skills gives you a feeling of capability, confidence and well-being. If you are doing what you really want to do most, work will feel like play, even though you may encounter and struggle with challenges in the process. This is a learning curve.

Healthy aggression is a way of asserting yourself, of being who you are. This is not at the expense of anyone else; nor is it demanding, both of which are self-centred. It is selfish in a positive way, because you do need to think about yourself and your needs. If you have not learned to contain your aggression, you may not respect other people, or their boundaries. You may channel aggression into bullying, to get what you want, rather than asking for it. If you have not been allowed to express healthy aggression through suitable activities and play as a child, you may be afraid to assert yourself now. You may be afraid to reach out for what you want, or you may use demanding behaviour because you do not know how to ask for, or expect to get, it.

Like making boundaries and expressing anger, assertion is a clear and clean way of saying who you are and what you want, without destructive aggression. You can assert yourself with love. If you do not believe in your right to assert yourself, you are more likely to bully.

Sexual Feelings

As I see it, there are three aspects to sexuality:

Sexuality is a biological urge to reproduce and a physical urge for pleasure and gratification. This biological and physical drive is felt through, often very urgent, sensations in your body, originating in your genitals but centred in your belly, from where you feel the urge to act on these feelings.

In humans, sexuality is also tempered with heart-centred feelings of love and joy and the urge to share these feelings with another. Sexuality is an expression, but not the only one available, of vitality, of lust for life; and a way of celebrating yourself, your partner and your relationship.

Sexuality is also a spiritual urge, a longing to unite with something greater than you; with what is divine, however you conceive of that divinity, although sexuality is not the only pathway to divinity. By uniting with something greater than you, you become more. This is the urge to expand and grow. Although it is generated by longing, felt in your heart, your conception of divinity is head-centred, close to the realm of vision and fantasy, but, just like your physical urges, it needs to be tempered through your heart. In this way, through love, sex becomes an act of worship of something that is sacred. Because it is sacred, it needs to be treated with respect.

In mature adults, these three aspects of sexuality can function together in balance; or they can be out of balance.

Like all urges, sexuality needs containing. However, you may act out sexually, purely on your physical, hormonal urges. This does not mean you are grown up, even though hormonal genital urges start at the age of physical maturity. Acting out sexually without your heart being engaged is sex without love and without considering the consequences. This is dangerous, self-centred and leads to pain.

Some children use the physical pleasure of genital stimulation to comfort themselves, which implies loneliness and pain. This is not mature sexuality. Engaging in genital stimulation, mutual or otherwise, that is, masturbation, that does not have a heart connection, is using sex as a painkiller, and using yourself or one another. This leaves you feeling empty and dissatisfied, and eventually in more pain. This is not the same as pleasuring yourself, when you also love yourself. Being without a partner need not mean you are in pain.

If you project your conception of divinity onto your partner, you are not making a heart connection with them; you are detached from them as a person. You are trying to make love with a spiritual fantasy. You cannot have sex through your head, even though fantasy can turn you on physically. If your heart is not involved, there is no love and, without love, you cannot connect to divinity, or to the person you are having sex with. You are using them. You are also having unrealistic expectations of them. There is a strong possibility of delusion, disappointment and dependency. In fact, you are using them as a reflection of your self, which is narcissistic. This kind of sexual relationship will not be satisfying or fulfilling, however good your physical technique is. You may worship (your fantasy of) the person you are having sex with, but this will not help you to love yourself, even though it may leave you feeling spiritual for a while. Eventually, you will be left feeling empty because you are not making a true connection to something greater than yourself, or even to another person. You can only reach beyond yourself through your heart, whether you do this with a partner or not. Nothing else is genuine.

Mature sexuality is a marriage of your genitals, body, head and heart, which includes your intelligence. As an adult, you do need to use this to check out who you are doing it with and whether that is appropriate, and safe. This is how you learn to contain your sexual feelings, so that you can make choices in relationships, so you can allow love, including self-love, to grow before you enter into sexual activity. If you do not use your intelligence to discriminate, there is a strong risk of rejection, intentional or not, at some time.

If you act out sexually without your heart being engaged, you are using the other person and abusing yourself. You may get gratification of your physical urges, physical pleasure, but you will not get satisfaction or fulfilment of your emotional and spiritual urges. If you use fantasy to turn you on, instead of your desire for one another, you will be disappointed; your sexual encounters will leave you feeling empty because, ultimately, you are having sex with yourself alone. This is not love, but longing. You may connect with the divinity in yourself because, after all, even lust is spiritual, it has your life force in it (unless it is used destructively); but you will not connect with the other person; nor will you share love; and you will not go beyond yourself, which we all need to do at times in order to gain meaning in our lives. Sexuality is not the only way to gain meaning but, if you are misusing sexuality in this way, it is unlikely you will find meaning in other aspects of your life.

> 'The highest and the lowest are always closest to each other in the sphere of sexuality.'
> – Sigmund Freud

Sexuality can be used as a way of avoiding or acting out many feelings that are not sexual at all. It may be used purely for recreation, for releasing aggression, tension or anxiety, or for attempting to kill pain, for comfort, to alleviate loneliness, or even for expressing hatred and vengeance or gaining feelings of power and control, but without forming relationships or understanding its true value and meaning. This can be addictive and destructive. You will know whether sexual activity is bringing you temporary relief from these feelings, or whether it is bringing you love, joy, spiritual connection and expansion. You will know whether it is enabling true self-expression, which leads to feelings of self-esteem and fulfilment, or whether it makes you feel bad about yourself. Anything that makes you feel this way is ultimately punishing, even if it is you who is doing this to yourself.

The purpose of mature sexuality is to create: offspring, love and greater meaning, all of which perpetuate the human race and enable us to grow and evolve as human beings. Sexuality may not be the only route to love and meaning, but it is a very pleasurable one when used appropriately and safely.

Many of you will have been given immature models of sexuality and many of you will have had your sexuality negated, rejected or even abused by fearful, jealous, disappointed, disillusioned, negative or immature parents, who either could not contain their own sexuality or were negating or suppressing and denying it. If your sexuality has been rejected, you may be stuck in competitiveness and dependency because you are afraid to take up the full power of your gender and sexuality in case this happens again. You may decline to grow up completely. After all, sexuality is the final gift of maturity, the last stage of growing up, and you do not want this gift to be destroyed. Because mature sexuality also involves your heart, you are vulnerable if you do not treat this most precious gift with care. If you own it, you then have the choice whether and how to use it. If you do not own it, you may find it using you.

Remember, all feelings, including sexual feelings, are healthy and natural, it is how you choose to use them that determines whether they are creative or destructive and what meaning they have for you. Any perversion of any feeling, including sexual perversion, will lead to pain. The paradox is that perversion is usually an attempt to avoid pain. This does not work. It is facing pain that ultimately frees you.

For You to Think About:

How you create love and pain in your life.
How you use your sexuality.

---

*'Many persons have a wrong idea of what constitutes true happiness.
It is not attained through self-gratification,
but through fidelity to a purpose.'
– Helen Keller*

Part III

Becoming More of Who You Are

13

KNOWING WHERE YOU'RE GOING

> *'Ordinary riches can be stolen,*
> *real riches cannot.*
> *In your soul are infinitely precious things*
> *that cannot be taken from you.'*
> *– Oscar Wilde*

Your Soul – Knowing and Claiming Who You Are

I have talked about gaining a sense of self. Your self is your soul, your essence; that part of you that is indestructible, whatever defences, including madness, you may adopt to deny it when it feels threatened. Your self is essentially good. You never truly compromise your self, you only hide it and adopt a false self, which you believe will serve you better in the circumstances you find yourself in and which you believe you cannot change. As an adult, you have far more ability to change your circumstances than you did as a child. Some people call your essence your inner child. I like to think of it as that personal spark of divinity within you, which is part of a greater divinity, to which you belong. You may understand this spark of divinity as your higher power and the greater divinity as God.

Although you were probably born with a good connection to your own essence, unless you were traumatised before or during birth, you can lose this over time if it is not respected, reflected and supported by the environment you grow up in. It is as if you forget who you are when you deny your self, which deadens you and often leads to illness, depression and *dis*-ease. Denial is unconscious, so you believe your false reality to be true. Because that identity never feels quite right for you, you believe there is something wrong with you. In essence, there is nothing wrong with you. It is the way you present yourself that is flawed, a set of ineffective strategies for expressing your true self.

Your self is your birthright. It is the gift you bring into this world with you, which is your purpose in potential. Until you have finished dealing with the essentials of growing up, it is more difficult to concentrate on this purpose. But, when you have developed:

- independence,
- a good sense of your self,
- the ability to define that self and stand up for it,
- integrity and authority,
- the ability to be authentic,
- to feel and to know your own reality,
- and to channel your emotions constructively,
- courage, willingness to open your heart and to take risks,
- and to truly give of yourself,
- and mature sexuality,

you then have the ability to fulfil your purpose. Finding and fulfilling your purpose is the best cure I know for adult dependency, addictions, feelings of longing and emptiness and the projection of your dreams onto other people. When you follow your own dreams, you do not try to live your life through other people. Self-gratification and all that goes with it loses its meaning and the fulfilment of your own life's purpose gives meaning to your life instead.

The Difference Between False Pride, Ego and Self

> 'True sanity entails, in one way or another,
> the dissolution of the normal ego,
> that false self competently adjusted to
> our alienated social reality.'
> – R.D. Laing

Ego is the word often used for the false pride and false self I have talked about. This is an empty, fragile and inflated pseudo-ego you might use to compensate for feelings of inferiority and poverty or for self-aggrandisement when you feel small and weak. It is that self-centred part of your personality that is needy and grasping, because you are afraid you do not have inner resources. In fact, by adopting false pride as a defence because you do not feel safe to express yourself, you cut yourself off from your resourceful self. You may have grown up believing you will be rejected, harmed or humiliated if you show who you really are. If you adopted a façade that prevented you feeling alienated in the society in which you grew, it will prevent you being accepted now for who you really are. This façade alienates you from yourself. You reject and abandon yourself.

Your soul needs a structure, in which to function and be effective, which is built by healthy growing up. It is a small, but well-formed, integrated ego, which I call personality. It grows as you grow. You use your personality to present your individuality, your self, and connect that self to the world you live in. It is *how* you go about *being* who you are. Ego is a gift of growing up, not something you want to get rid of, like false pride. Without an ego you are impotent and faceless. If your personality is aligned with your self, because you are conscious of that self, your ego will work for and not against you. Your personality helps you to be more of who you are, to express yourself and to share yourself with other people. Unfortunately, as a child, it tends to adapt to your environment more than it adapts to your self. Hopefully, you have grown up in a loving, accepting and supportive environment, which has helped your soul to flourish and your personality to form in harmony with that soul.

However, if your personality is adapted to an alien reality and not in harmony with your soul, your behaviour will be self-defeating, dependent, aloof and possibly addictive, because adapting prevents you from growing up. You feel split and at odds with yourself. Your behaviour does not match who you feel yourself to be, deep inside. You never have real peace. If you work to refine your personality by acting with integrity and listening to your conscience, you will become conscious of your denial of your true self. Then you will be able to tap your innate soul's wisdom, which ultimately guides you, and to find and fulfil your purpose.

Examining Your Beliefs and Retrieving Your Dreams

> *'To dream anything that you want to dream,*
> *that is the beauty of the human mind.*
> *To do anything that you want to do,*
> *that is the strength of the human will.*
> *To trust yourself, to test your limits,*
> *that is the courage to succeed.'*
> *– Bernard Edmonds*

Your dreams are your heart's desires. That means you *feel* them as convictions. They are what you long for and what you believe in. They are embedded in your soul and therefore indestructible and in harmony with your will. Your will is your soul's purpose.

When you add love and courage to will and desire, they become joy and devotion, the basis of true vocation. Love, courage, will, desire, joy and devotion are all heart-centred. Fulfilling your dreams means living your life as vocation – with heart. Part of vocation is the work you do to earn your living. The rest is merely how you live your life, in harmony with your true calling, the voice of guidance you hear inside you, when you listen to your heart.

> *Will without love becomes wilfulness and*
> *desire without love becomes greed and self-centredness.*

Some questions:

- Try examining your beliefs to see if they are true to your self.
- Do you *feel* them, as conviction or *think* them as opinions?
- Are they beliefs you have acquired in order to make sense of and fit into the world you grew up in?
- Have you adapted your dreams accordingly?
- Do you believe your dreams are impossible?
- Are they rooted in your heart's desires?

Your dreams have probably not been lost, but buried under a pile of erroneous beliefs and distorted thinking.

> *Faith and trust are the mediators
> between visualisation and materialisation.*

You can make your dreams real. However, if they have been denied, you may inflate them out of proportion and get anxious because they feel overwhelming and unmanageable. You will need to ground them in your present reality, put them into the perspective of your life, hold them and allow them to grow over time. You will also need to protect them from the jealousy of others and your own destructiveness. It may be that your dreams were never held for you as a child, or were rubbished by others through their own bitterness. Dreams have a way of falling flat if you try to push them and visions can come to harm if your expose them before they are fully materialised.

Your dreams have a process of their own. Just as you once did, they need patience, endurance, courage and perseverance, as well as love and acceptance to nurture them until they are fully grown. This also means allowing uncertainty and taking considered risks.

> *'Love is the light that illuminates the path.'*
> *– Dane Rudhyar*

Walking Your Path with Love

You hold your visions in your mind, your imagination. The impulse to act on them comes from your belly centre, the place of wilfulness, which is fine, because, without this drive, you would not materialise them. After all, it is selfishness that motivates you; your dreams are for your own fulfilment and self-satisfaction. But it is through love that the process is refined so that what you do is also altruistic. Your heart is the seat of faith and trust, conviction, courage, commitment and true belief. When you *feel* your convictions, you know you are on the right track. Convictions are different to opinions, which are thoughts, not feelings. However, you can use your intellect to interpret and articulate what you feel in your heart.

> *Remember:*
> *You do not have to be limited by the limitations*
> *of previous generations.*

But also remember with gratitude the gifts you have inherited from your forebears, even if they did not have the opportunities that you have to develop them fully.

It is helpful to link with like-minded people who share your dreams and ideals. This helps you to find your niche in life and a sense of belonging. Your path need not be lonely. You will touch many people on your personal path if it is one of love, rather than greed and self-gratification.

> *'If we walk*
> *The true way*
> *In our inmost heart,*
> *Even without praying,*
> *God will be with us!'*
> *– Takuan Soho*

It is when you align your will, that spark of God or divinity within you, with your soul's purpose that you truly walk your path in harmony and resolve your inner conflict. Then you are less likely to have conflict in your relationships. You have the confidence that comes from knowing your own heart. Because you believe in your self, you love yourself and are more likely to generate love around you. This path is a lifelong process of unfolding and growing. It is a path with heart; a spiritual, as well as material, path. Any spiritual path needs to be grounded in the reality of every day life. Otherwise it is an attempt to escape from that life.

It is unlikely that you will live life free of conflict, but, if you are used to being true to your self, you will know where to look for solutions. You can ask yourself:

- What you are denying.
- What part of your self you are hiding;
- And why?
- What the threat is;
- And if it is real or imaginary?
- If false pride is holding you back and;
- Decide how to integrate this part of you into your life,
- Find it expression.

When you let go of false pride, it is like stepping into rhythm with the universe. Then the universe responds and supports you, dances with you. Your life flows smoothly. You have a sense of having put down a large burden, which is your resistance. Why resist your own soul's desires? You are more likely to do this if they have been thwarted, negated or denigrated during your upbringing. You will not always get what you want, but you will get what you need to fulfil your purpose. That will make you feel contented.

Your dreams represent your ambitions. There is no harm in being ambitious, as long as it is not at the expense of anyone else, which it need not be; and as long as the ambition is yours and not your parents', or a reaction against their ambitions for you, both of which may not be true to you. You are entitled to your achievements. But you do not have to prove anything to anybody. You are entitled to do what you want to do most, if it comes from that place of conviction, in your heart. No one can take that away from you. It is self-defeating to deny it.

Do not confuse ambition with competition. You may be tempted to compete simply for the sake of competitiveness, to inflate your false ego. Why compete for something you do not want anyway, or something you already have but are not owning? True pride will come from fulfilling your personal ambitions.

Creativity Is Work and Play

> 'Our deepest fear is not that we are inadequate.
> Our deepest fear is that we are powerful beyond measure.
> It is our Light, not our Darkness, that most frightens us.'
> – Marianne Williamson

Anxiety blocks creativity. As a mixture of work and play, like following your path, your creativity needs thinking, feeling and doing, as well as a little intuition, so that it is focussed, safe and constructive. Your spontaneity needs containing and managing, just as a child's play needs boundaries and security. Then you can work passionately at what you choose to do; expressing your joy and power creatively. If you believe your creative power is unacceptable, or that you are unacceptable, you will be afraid to re-create yourself in your work and play. You will turn frustrated creativity outwards as violence or inwards, self-destructively.

Creativity is inspired by your soul and its response to external stimuli. Inspiration needs work to bring it to materialisation and completion. Some of this work may be mundane and boring, but it furthers your purpose. I believe that work, when done creatively, is very similar to play. It is essential to your nature to play. That is why it is important that you do work that is fulfilling, that uses your potential, stimulates your creativity and is aligned with your soul's purpose; work that stretches you on all levels.

> 'If you do not feel yourself growing in your work
> and your life broadening and deepening,
> if your task is not a perpetual tonic to you,
> you have not found your place.'
> – Orison Swett Marden

Work is not something you have to suffer to get rewards or to endure until you have time off for recreation. Work is something you can do for pleasure and re-creation. You might then consider non-working time as rest.

Finding Meaning and Purpose

> 'There is no meaning to life
> except the meaning man gives to his life
> by the unfolding of his powers.'
> – Erich Fromm

Since love is your essence, your purpose is to express it in whatever way moves you. Then your life will have meaning, without which it feels empty. You may try to fill it from outside yourself, giving meaning to things that do not reflect who you are, but reflect or compensate for negative feelings about yourself or support your false ego, your façade. You can fill yourself up with dependent relationships, with activities like gossiping, other people's concerns, or with emotions like competitiveness and hatred. You can fill yourself up with achievement for the sake of achievement, rather than for the sake of fulfilment. These are all poor substitutes for love. Using spirituality as a means of escape from your false reality will not connect you to something greater if you are not first connected to your self through love; nor will you find greater meaning if you have no meaning in your life. None of this will fulfil your purpose.

When you give meaning to your world by living soulfully, objects and people in your life do not fill you up; they express who you already are. You gain meaning from a world that reflects your true self, rather than your false pride. Fulfilling your purpose is likely to have more meaning if it is based on what you feel you want most, rather than on what you believe or have been taught you ought to want. You build only illusions around such beliefs and therefore a life that does not suit you at all. It lets you down.

You have not grown up without outside influences. There will be times when you lose direction. There will be some struggle, some suffering and some sacrifices. You will have to adapt, to change direction at times, especially when you take diversions and go off on tangents, as is possible or even probable. This struggle, suffering and sacrifice adds meaning to your process and helps you to clarify your purpose, to remake your commitment to it   from time to time.

It also helps you to form your own philosophy by which to live your life, which grows sounder as you grow up. Your philosophy is more likely to be sound if it is based on a genuine response to how you are received in the world, than if it is based on a reaction to the world's reception of your false self.

Becky Became a Healer

Becky's mother's ambition was for her to be a doctor. She had also brought her up to expect to get married and have children. Becky's father said they could not afford to send Becky to university. Becky thought she wanted to be a linguist because she was good at languages. She was dissuaded by the school careers counsellor and advised to train to be a teacher or a secretary. This did not appeal. Becky was impatient to become independent, so she left school early and took a job that enabled her to train in computing skills, at which she did well over the years. She was able to command a large salary.

After leaving school, Becky developed eczema, then asthma, and later a small cancer. When she came to see me, she had learned a lot about alternative medicines, which had healed these conditions, but she was suffering from the beginnings of an arthritic condition. She told me she was finding it more and more difficult to make herself go to work and, although she was very good at what she did, her work and its setting felt increasingly alien to her. She felt she was living a lie.

An alternative doctor friend of Becky's believed she had considerable healing abilities. Becky also had a lover who had asked her to marry him. When I suggested she married, gave up her job, retrained to be a healer and had a child, she wept with relief. She said she felt she had been given permission at last to be herself; but she was afraid of giving up her independence. She would be financially dependent on her husband. Realising this she expressed a great deal of anger towards her father, who had failed to support or finance her education. She began to respect her mother's intuition, even though her vision was limited to what information had been available to her at that time.

Becky did marry her man and have a child, after which her arthritis abated. She enjoyed keeping house and, when her daughter started school, she realised her ambition to go to university. She studied psychology. She became an excellent healer and therapist and was happy doing what she wanted to do most.

Money and How You Value Yourself

As an adult, you have the ability to earn money and use it as you wish, which you mainly could not do as a child.
Money, earned purposefully, serves love, not greed. It:

- Is a benefit of fulfilling your purpose, not the purpose of your work.
- Gives value to what you do, but is not a substitute for meaning.
- Rewards your power, but does not give you power.
- Gives you pleasure rather than gratification.

> *'It is too difficult to think nobly when one thinks only of earning a living.'*
> *– Jean-Jacques Rousseau*

It is also difficult to think nobly when you are hungry and need a roof over your head. But it is possible to be realistic about what you can do with the gifts you have, how you can nurture and develop those gifts and how you can have their value reflected in payment for the work you do. This starts by knowing your own worth and believing in it. Of course, you may have to develop your gifts by acquiring skills and training.

> *Spiritual freedom requires material security*

For You to Think About:

Your heart's desires.
How you value yourself.

> *'Ecstasy is living with the soul in the body.'*
> *– Chris Griscom*

14

ALL COMPLETE AND PERFECT

> *Love is your shield, truth your integrity,*
> *and anger, your right, to protect you.*
> *Demanding the truth means being honest with yourself.*
> *Wanting to be trusted means trusting yourself.*

Living In a State of Grace

Grace is a state of loving kindness, goodwill, gratitude and acceptance. When you live honestly, with integrity, with your soul truly embodied, with meaning in your life, your spirit alive, and have created the safety of love around you; when you know how to make boundaries and trust your inner divinity, your higher power, or what you understand as God, and you have faith that there is something that is bigger than you of which you are a part, and to which you feel connected, you are in a state of grace.

In this state of grace you:

- feel at one with yourself, the universe and the world around you.
- accept yourself and others.
- are grateful for all you have.
- have a sense of connection and continuity
- yet you live in the present, not the past or the future.
- believe and have faith in your heart's desires and listen to your conscience.

If you follow a spiritual discipline, it is one that is aligned to your own heart, your will and purpose. You do not follow blindly. Your spirituality becomes your source of discipline.

When you are in a state of grace, you have no false pride because you have let go and grieved the props that supported your inflated ego – grown out of them, and no longer look to other people to reflect who you are. Being free of myths, misconceptions, guilt, fears, onerous burdens and confusion and therefore conscious and aware, you are able to experience clarity and serenity and to have peace of mind. You have grown up spiritually. This, I believe, is being enlightened.

Having resolved you inner confusion by moving through fear and pain to the purity of your own soul, having reclaimed your spirit from deadening emotions, you are able to see what experiences disturb your serenity and confuse you; and to avoid them when you can. It is more likely you will choose experiences that align with your inner, clear and serene, experience of yourself. You know that it is OK for you to say no to experiences that are unhealthy or crazy-making, that distract you from your own reality and make you feel unreal or dysfunctional. Now you are at the centre of your own life, grounded in your own reality and take responsibility for what happens to you without blaming. You clarify your intentions and make them good. Because you experience your essential goodness and like being with yourself, you do not feel lonely. You are free from hatred and negativity because, rather than run away from it, you have confronted your own, come to understand it and what can cause it. Having challenged hatred and transformed it back into good, into love, you understand that it is, in fact, perverted and misguided love. By loving yourself, you are able to live with serenity amidst life's challenges and tensions. They do not shake you. Nor do you avoid them. You see life as it really is and deal with it. Your life becomes less effort, more joyful, because you are no longer resisting it and have said 'yes' to yourself and all you are. Because you are in touch with your own divinity, you see and choose to relate with what is divine in others and no longer fear, judge or look for faults in them; only for love.

Grace is not a life of constant bliss, but it is a life of healing. You learn how to heal yourself. It is possible that others will find your presence healing too. Moments of ecstasy occur, which are closer to serenity than the highs you may have experienced through addictive behaviours. There are lows too, but they are far more transient than you may have experienced before.

Your grown up spirituality will be effective, in your daily life. It becomes a philosophy that you live by, not one you necessarily preach. It becomes love in action, not inaction. It is an effective love, not a passive love, because it has your will and heart's desire behind it. Your life is not passive because you have reclaimed healthy lust for life, vitality and spirit.

Remaining Youthful

If you embody your soul, your essential nature, you remain childlike, but not childish. You retain an innocence Suzuki calls 'beginner's mind', even when you have expertise.

> *'In the beginner's mind there are many possibilities,*
> *but in the experts there are few.'*
> *– Shunryu Suzuki*

Your mind is flexible and always open to new and varied possibilities. You are not ashamed to admit what you do not know. You know how to learn and are open to new experience and change, whatever age you are. If you close your mind, you stagnate. By keeping your mind open, you keep it young and fresh. This is how you retain youthfulness throughout your life, even when your body ages.

Attaining Simplicity and Humility

> *'A person's errors are his portals of discovery.'*
> *– James Joyce*

When you accept your mistakes graciously, and learn from them, you learn humility. This is different from humiliation, when someone else shames you. Humility is a choice. It is an antidote to false pride, which is a reaction to humiliation. So accepting rejections as the other person's choice also keeps you humble. Humility fills you up from inside, so you no longer feel needy and greedy. You are happy with simplicity. You learn that living simply makes you life easier. Letting go of the trappings of self-aggrandisement and gratification makes you feel lighter, more graceful. This is the meaning of 'enlightenment.' You are setting down a heavy burden and reserving vital energy for more creative pursuits that bring you pleasure, fulfilment and diversity. You have more time in your life for what really matters to you, for your soul's desires. You no longer chase glamour, fame and glory, but accept them with humility if they come to you and if they are appropriate.

Being in a state of grace, you learn to believe that, if you are completely clear about what you want, it will come to you very quickly. You take care to only ask for what you need for your soul's journey. You travel lightly, clearing out your inner clutter. You do not clog up your life with dross and negativity, gossip and rumour, or with activities that feed an inflated ego. You value beauty and have as much of it in your life as you can manage.

You Never Stop Growing

> *'If every day is an awakening,*
> *you will never grow old.*
> *You will just keep growing.'*
> *– Gail Sheehy*

The trick is to stay fresh. Just as you need to use your head, heart and body in union to walk your path with love, and thinking, feeling and doing in creative work and play, so you need to keep all three functions alive and working in harmony throughout your life in order to remain in a state of grace. Take care to listen to conflict and resolve it. Sometimes what you think may clash with what you feel, or what your body wants to do. At these times I find it useful to set up an imaginary dialogue between my head, heart and body (belly) and let them negotiate. In this way you can tap your innate wisdom. You can take one day at a time, knowing you will make enough space in your life for all your needs.

Your body will age, but that is no reason not to treat it with care and respect. After all, it is the vehicle that enables your soul to act in this world. So diet, movement, exercise and rest keep your body alive and vital, loving keeps your heart open and gives you hope and joy, and learning keeps your mind active, fresh and young. In this way you move through your world more gracefully. If you have youthfulness, you will not be chasing lost youth. You will use your sexuality appropriately. As you grow older, you will grow 'up' instead of growing 'down', regressing to dependency, shrinking and deteriorating.

Aging Need Not Mean Illness and Infirmity

> *'Of all the self-fulfilling prophecies in our culture,*
> *the assumption that aging means decline and poor health*
> *is probably the deadliest.'*
> *– Marilyn Ferguson*

It is possible, as you grow through your life, to gain grace and wisdom, which means that, as your physical strength declines, your mental and spiritual abilities increase. It is more likely that you will become ill and infirm if you do not nurture all your faculties and attend to all your needs, especially for creativity, self-expression, purpose, meaning, love and connection. If you remain sad, bitter, angry, resentful, frustrated and disappointed as you age, you are more likely to decline in health. These emotions accumulate, stagnate, fester and foster dis-ease, a semi-illness that comes from emotional unease. You may not notice this so much when you are younger and have more energy for denial, (which takes a lot of energy), for activities that help you avoid your reality, use up your aggression and kill pain. You may act out then, but that is not working through.

You probably will have less physical strength and more emotional strength, more strength of character, as you age, but, if you have attained a state of grace, you will know how to use this strength to its best advantage. You may have more physical strength when you are younger, but you are also more likely to waste it. At the end of the day, you will be able to assess your life not by the age you attain, but by what you have done with the years you have had. It is better to have truly lived for fewer years, than to have existed for many with little vitality or value in them. Much of the latter part of your life will be a reflection of how you have lived earlier, although it is never too late to make changes.

From Indignation to Dignity

Dignity comes from feeling sacred, that is special, precious and dedicated to your purpose; and holy, which means sound, whole and healthy, spiritually pure and deserving of respect and reverence. If you are seen this way as a child, you will grow up with dignity. You will be aligned with your self and your purpose and live mainly in a state of balance, having inner peace, which shows on the outside. You will be dignified and command respect. If you are abused and shamed as a child, you grow up with indignation. You are less likely to respect yourself. Nor can you be dignified if you are carrying the burden of guilt.

Dignity comes from pride in yourself and in your achievements; in who you are and what you do. You are entitled to feel proud of both. It comes from taking possession of your self and being your own person, with pride. As you become your own person, you let go of guilt. You consult your own conscience, rather than the inappropriate rules you were given in the form of punishments and judgements. You learn to use your own judgement, that guilt is a useless emotion, and that it only serves the aggrandisement of someone else. You no longer need to shore up other people's egos in the hope they will approve of you. You approve of yourself now. Because you value yourself, you feel worthy. This gives you poise, self-respect and self-esteem. Because you are honest, your have nothing to feel ashamed of; you can hold your head up – without stiffening your neck. You have taken possession of your sexuality and know yourself as a man or a woman. You feel whole, complete and self-contained. You conduct yourself in a dignified manner, which is not aloof or unreachable. You are warm, kind and approachable, (but may not suffer fools gladly).

> 'He who hurries can not walk with dignity.'
> – Chinese Proverb

If you are still carrying rage and pain, you do not feel dignified. You feel indignant. For most people, it takes time to let go of rage and pain from your past. You need to identify what is bringing you down and undermining you, understand what happened to you, hand back responsibility and move on. You need to let go of blame from the past and take responsibility for your own life now.

Forgiveness and Gratitude

> 'You will know that forgiveness has begun
> when you recall those who hurt you
> and feel the power to wish them well.'
> – Lewis B Smedes

When you forgive your enemy, you disarm them. They no longer have power over you. There is no one to blame. As long as you hold a grudge, you give them power they do not have. You are their victim. You invest a part of your energy in them and have less for yourself. Your grudge does more harm to you than it does to your enemy; bitterness grows inside you and festers. Forgiveness heals you and sets you free. You reclaim your power to love.

Forgiveness is for yourself, so that you will feel better. You can forgive people, even if you do not forgive behaviours. And you may not forget those behaviours either, but you can understand them and learn from them, acknowledge what part you had to play in them and how you might have acted differently, with hindsight. Forgiveness helps you to stand in your enemies' shoes, to have empathy and compassion, to understand their motivations. It is important not to let resentment fester because, as long as it continues to live in you, you will not be free. You can have neither grace nor dignity. Forgiving ends the pain you carry around with you and add to, pain on pain, until you forgive and let it go. Forgiveness frees you from fear of what has hurt you in the past. It makes you world safer because you no longer carry ill will or have enemies. When you forgive you make your life more beautiful. You make yourself feel younger. It is forgiveness that enables you to channel your energies into positive, rather than negative directions and to live in the present.

Forgiveness is a kind of internal hygiene, but it is important not to forgive before you are ready. You need to feel, then to understand and then to let go. Forgiveness is empty if you do not feel it and will not heal you if you use it as a means of denial. Then it is not genuine. You need to feel it, not just think it.

When you have forgiven, you can be grateful for the love in your life, for all the gifts that you do have and for lessons learned from your enemies, who are often your best teachers. At the end of each day, I find it helpful to think about the goodness that day has brought me, what I have gained, what lessons I have learned and what I have achieved. I offer up a prayer of gratitude. This helps me to forgive the hurts and disappointments, which are inevitable, so that I do not carry grudges into the next day.

The Story of an Abuse Survivor

> Precious came to see me after a close male friend died. We worked through the normal process of grief, but she seemed to be talking more and more about her relationship with her father, who, she told me, had raped her when she was an adolescent. Her mother was away at the time, recovering from a long illness. She also told me she had done a lot of recovery work on her sexual abuse.
>
> I encouraged Precious to express her anger and to grieve for the innocent child she had been before she was violated. Her response to this was to tell me she no longer felt like a victim. Instead of expressing anger and pain, she expressed her gratitude at having survived her ordeal. She told me she was proud of herself and felt stronger and more beautiful after all she had been through. She said she had never expressed these feelings before and felt like she had 'come out' at last. She was no longer hiding beneath shame and humiliation. She felt able to forgive her father, but not what he did.
>
> She also expressed gratitude for her strong, supportive, male friend, who had loved her unconditionally, even though they had never been lovers. Her memory of him renewed her trust in men and enabled her to see her father, not as an evil man, but as a weak one.

She said that my ability to be there for her had enabled her to finally come to terms with the rape because her mother had not been there for her when it happened and was too weak and fragile for Precious to confide in her afterwards. I reminded her she had already done a lot of work facing her pain, shame, anger and guilt. She agreed. Precious was ready to let go of her past. She walked away with pride and dignity.

Facing Your Mortality

> 'Death is like a mirror
> in which the true meaning of life is reflected.'
> – Sogyal Rinpoche

This book has been about how you can live your life to its full advantage. When you have grace and dignity and have forgiven your enemies, you can face your own mortality. This is a humbling experience, to know and accept that you are not finite, or omnipotent, that you do not have ultimate control of your life, but also that you do have choices in how you can live it and in how you might die, when the time is right. Even if your death is sudden and unpredictable, you can prepare for it even now, not morbidly, but joyfully. If your life has been a loving experience, then so is your death likely to be. Just as you have learned to accept change and uncertainty, one day you will learn to accept the fact of your mortality. This acceptance gives greater meaning to your life and how you choose to live it.

You might like to think of death as just another transition, letting go, changing, transforming and moving on.

For You to Think About:

Your dignity.
How you forgive.

> '*And as we let our light shine,*
> *We unconsciously give other people permission to do the same.*
> *As we are liberated from our own fear,*
> *Our presence automatically liberates others.*'
> *– Marianne Williamson*

Lightning Source UK Ltd.
Milton Keynes UK
UKOW02f1543271216
290817UK00001B/17/P